A Maker's Mindset

30 LESSONS FROM THE LATHE

Martin Saban-Smith RPT

Published by:

Woodturning Online Limited
Garthowen Garden Centre
Alton Lane
Four Marks
Hampshire
GU34 5AJ
United Kingdom

ISBN 978-1-0683581-2-8

First Edition

www.msabansmith.com
www.thewoodturning.school
www.woodturning360.com

Demonstrating at a tool shop in 2019.

Before We Begin

THIS ISN'T A technical manual.

You won't find tool specifications, project plans, or step-by-step instructions for turning specific pieces. Plenty of excellent books already do that work, and I've learnt from a few of them.

This book is about what I've learnt. Not just about turning, though there's plenty of that here. But about making in the broader sense: what it asks of us, what it gives back, how it changes the person doing it. The title, "A Maker's Mindset," reflects my belief that how you think about the work matters as much as how you execute it. Technique without philosophy produces competent emptiness. Philosophy without technique produces well-meaning failure. You need both.

I came to woodturning late. I was in my late thirties, had spent decades as a photographer and designer, and thought I understood making. I come from a very creative family that has dipped in and out of crafts for as long as I can remember. Then I stood at a lathe for the first time and realised I knew nothing at all.

That was 2014. In the years since, I've turned thousands of pieces, started a YouTube channel (like thousands of others), demonstrated internationally, started a finishes business, founded a school, taught hundreds of students, written a book about form and proportion, and somehow become someone people ask for advice. None of this was planned. I just kept showing up at the lathe, kept paying attention, kept trying to understand what the wood and the work were teaching me.

The book is organised into five main parts, moving from Hands to Mind to Heart to Meaning to Legacy. You can read it straight through, which is how I'd suggest approaching it first. But you can also dip in wherever draws you. Each section stands alone while connecting to the larger whole. Some days you need "The Weight of Patience." Other days you need "Happy Accidents." This book will meet you where you are.

A note on who this is for: I've written primarily for woodturners, because that's my craft and my community. If you work with your hands, if you shape a material into a form, if you care about doing something well for its own sake, you'll find yourself in these pages. The lathe is a great teacher, but the lessons are universal.

I should mention that I'm a deep and chaotic thinker. My mind works in spirals rather than straight lines, making connections between things that seem unrelated, revisiting ideas from new angles. You'll notice this in the writing. Stories interrupt theory. If you prefer linear instruction, this may occasionally frustrate you. Sorry about that, but I've found that craft knowledge rarely travels in straight lines anyway. It spirals, returns, deepens with each pass. Perhaps that's fitting for a book about working on a lathe.

This book is published in the year of my fiftieth birthday, so perhaps writing this is a half-century brain-dump, expressing what I've learnt about life through the craft of woodturning. You decide, but I hope you enjoy it and gain insight into your own journey from the thirty lessons within these pages.

I owe debts to more people than I can name. Every turner I've watched, every student who asked a question, every piece of wood that refused to cooperate, every maker who shared their knowledge freely: all of them contributed to whatever understanding I've managed to gather. The tradition carries us. We carry it forward.

Finally, a request. If something in this book helps you, pass it on. Show someone how to sharpen. Demonstrate a technique at your club. Share what you've learnt with someone just starting out. The knowledge in these pages isn't just mine. It came from others and it should continue to others. That's how traditions survive. That's how the circle continues.

Now. The blank is waiting. The tools are sharp.

Let's begin.

Martin Saban-Smith RPT

Hampshire, 2026

A student's first day at the lathe at The Woodturning School.

Part One

What the Hands Know

Before you can think about turning, your hands must learn it. These first six lessons are about the physical foundations: the initial courage to begin, the search for balance and centre, the conversation with grain, the relationship with tools, the discipline of sharpening, and the wisdom hidden in pauses. These are the bedrock everything else rests on. Master turners still work on these fundamentals because the hands never stop learning, never stop refining what they know.

1: The First Cut

FOR BEGINNERS, AND many more experienced turners, there is a moment just before the first cut when hesitation creeps in. The blank sits on the lathe, rough and silent, and you stand there with the gouge poised, wondering if you're about to make something beautiful or destroy something that could have been. That hesitation is the first obstacle every maker meets when they start learning. The only way through it is to *begin.*

I see this moment in every new student who comes to the school. They've prepared, they've probably watched lots of videos on social media, and they've imagined this moment. The lathe turns on and now the wood is spinning and the tool is in their hands. Suddenly the gap between knowing and doing feels enormous. Some freeze entirely. Others rush forward quickly. Both responses come from the same place: the fear is that this first cut will reveal something they'd rather not know about their own abilities.

But here's what I've learnt from watching hundreds of people make their first cuts: the quality of that cut matters far less than the act of making it in the first place. Those first rough cuts are ugly. They should be. You have to create a mess before you can create the form.

Beginning is courage disguised as clumsiness. The first cut doesn't have to be good. It just has to happen. Once you've made that first cut, everything changes. The wood is no longer precious. It's workable. You've entered into a dialogue with the material, and that's where all the learning lives.

There is a peculiar magic in that transition from thinking to doing. For weeks, months, sometimes years, we can carry ideas in our heads. Ideas don't teach you anything. Action does. The moment the gouge touches the wood, theory meets reality, and that friction is where growth happens.

This is true beyond the workshop too. How many plans remain perpetually unrealised because we're waiting for the perfect moment to begin? The novel that stays outlined but unwritten? The dream holiday that stays in the travel brochure? The conversation that stays rehearsed but unspoken? We tell ourselves we're preparing, but often we're just avoiding the vulnerability of beginning.

The lesson of the first cut is this: Readiness is a myth. You'll probably never feel completely prepared and ready, never have all the knowledge you think you need, never be certain of the outcome. If you wait for certainty, you'll wait forever.

The next phase is the hardest: that single moment before action. This is where resistance lives. The blank is mounted, the tools are sharp, but your hand hesitates. What if it goes wrong? What if I ruin this beautiful piece of wood? What if I'm not good enough yet? These questions loop endlessly if you let them. The only answer is to begin.

Once you make that first cut, everything shifts. The questions don't disappear, but they change. Instead of asking "What if I ruin it?" you start asking "How can I work with this?" The focus moves from judgement to observation, from fear to fascination.

Every new piece of wood is a dialogue you haven't had yet. You don't know exactly how it will respond, whether the grain will cooperate or surprise you, whether your vision will match reality. That uncertainty is part of the pleasure. If you knew exactly how everything would turn out, you'd be manufacturing, not making.

Learning to turn is about embracing the tools and

discovering what shapes you can make with them. That's where the learning lives. If you approach your first pieces with a fixed design in mind, expecting the wood to conform exactly to what you've imagined, frustration comes quickly. The gap between vision and result feels like failure.

But if you approach the lathe simply wanting to make a shape, the pressure lifts[1]. The piece might not match some imagined ideal, but you made something. It exists where an hour ago, it didn't. Your hands guided the tools through the wood, and a form emerged. That's not failure. That's the beginning of everything. The frustration that comes from imperfect results is softened by the pleasure of having made something for the first time. One approach sets you up for disappointment. The other sets you up for discovery.

This is true in teaching too. When a new student makes their first cut, they learn as much about themselves as they learn about the wood. Some approach tentatively, barely touching the surface, afraid to commit. Others dive in with too much confidence, pushing too hard, taking too much material. Both approaches teach important lessons.

The tentative cutter learns that wood is forgiving. They make a pass so light it barely marks the surface, then look up surprised that nothing terrible occurred. So they try again, a little bolder. The wood responds. They begin to understand that the material wants to be worked, that it will meet them halfway if they're willing to engage.

The bold cutter learns something different. They come in with energy and enthusiasm, but they haven't yet learnt that confidence without control creates problems. The wood will push back, catch the tool, remind them that this partnership requires respect. I've watched students take an aggressive first cut only to have the gouge grab and skate across the surface (and sometimes worse). The surprise on their faces is always the same. But that catch teaches them more about tool control in one second than ten minutes of explanation ever could.

Neither approach is wrong. Both are part of the learning process. What matters is that they've started, and that they're paying attention to what happens next.

Consider two approaches to learning. One person stands at the lathe for several minutes, gouge hovering, mentally rehearsing. They make one tentative pass, step back, and evaluate. By the time they've made three cuts, five minutes have passed. Meanwhile, the person at the next lathe has made twenty cuts in the same time. Some were good, some were terrible, but all of them provided information.

The person who made three cuts has learnt almost nothing because they've done almost nothing. They've spent their time in their head, not in the material. The person who made twenty cuts gains more experience[2]. Their body has started to learn what their mind could only imagine.

This isn't an argument for recklessness. Safety matters, preparation matters, thought matters. But there's a point where preparation becomes procrastination (I'm terrible at this), where caution becomes fear. The first cut draws that line. Before it, you're preparing. After it, you're working.

Here's what helps when fear holds you back: use cheap wood. Offcuts, firewood, anything you won't mourn if it goes wrong. When the material costs little, the stakes drop. You stop protecting the wood and start learning from it.

At the workshop, we keep plenty of board-ends and offcuts for this sort of thing. Want to see what happens when you push a bit harder? Try it on scrap. Curious about a different tool angle? Scrap. Worried you'll ruin something? You can't ruin something that was heading for the fire anyway.

This removes the preciousness that makes beginners hesitant. When the wood doesn't matter so much, you can focus on what your hands are learning rather than what you might lose. The cuts become experiments rather than performances. And somewhere in those experiments, confidence builds. Not false confidence from ignoring good practice, but real confidence from repetition on material you're free to explore without consequence.

Save the good wood for when you've earned it. Learn on the stuff that doesn't matter.

There's a moment in every turning where the piece looks its worst. It comes after the first rough cuts, when the form is marked out but not refined, when the shape is rough and uneven, when nothing appears to be beautiful. This is when discouragement often strikes. But this is the necessary stage. You can't get to the refined form without passing through the rough one. It's part of the process.

The first cut begins that process. It takes you from the safety of the imagined perfect piece to the reality of the imperfect work in progress. That's uncomfortable, but it's essential. Perfection exists only in the mind. In the physical world, everything is a series of approximations moving toward a goal that may shift as you work.

Remember: those videos were made by people who have possibly completed thousands of pieces. You're seeing the refined end of a very long process. Your first cut won't, and shouldn't, look like someone else's thousandth. It should look like a first cut: rough, exploratory, learning as it goes. That's appropriate. Honest. The way forward.

There's also a social dimension to the first cut that matters in a workshop setting. When one person starts, it gives the others permission and confidence. The first sound of wood meeting steel breaks the silence, and suddenly everyone feels less self-conscious about making noise, making mistakes, making anything. The workshop comes to life, and I love it.

The first catch, that jarring moment when the tool bites and the wood protests loudly, actually helps everyone relax. It breaks the illusion that everyone else is doing perfectly. It normalises difficulty. The first cut, and the first mistake, are communal gifts.

So here's what I tell every new student: *The first cut doesn't have to be perfect. It doesn't even have to be good. It just has to be. Make it with intention, with curiosity, with a willingness to learn from whatever happens next. Everything else grows from that simple act of beginning.*

The blank is waiting. The tools are sharp. The only question is: when will you start?

For me, the answer is always the same: *now.*

2: Finding Centre

THERE IS A peculiar irony about woodturning that took me years to understand. I thought the hardest part would be the technical work: mastering the cuts, learning to read grain, developing the hand-eye coordination that lets you coax a form from a spinning blank. All of that matters, of course. But the challenge that has caused me more trouble than any difficult timber or ambitious design is something far more fundamental: arriving at the workshop 'properly'.

Not physically arriving. That part is easy. You walk through the door, you switch on the lights, you look at the blank waiting on the bench. Physically, you're there. But whether you've actually arrived, whether you're truly present and ready to work, is another question entirely.

I learnt this the expensive way. Several years ago, I was preparing pieces with the idea of selling them. There was a relatively tight deadline, ambitious list, everything needed to go right. I'd had a frustrating morning, nothing to do with turning, just the ordinary chaos of life. But instead of acknowledging that chaos and doing something about it, I went straight to the lathe. The blank was mounted. The tools were sharp. I was ready to work.

Except I wasn't. My body was in the workshop but my mind was still replaying the other stuff I'd had going on earlier, still composing the email I should have written, still churning through problems I couldn't solve while standing at a lathe. The first bowl went badly. Not catastrophically, just poorly. The curves didn't flow. The proportions felt off. I pushed through anyway, telling myself it would come together in the finishing. It didn't.

The second piece was worse. I caught the tool because I wasn't being respectful of what I was doing. I was thinking about what I'd been doing earlier, somewhere else entirely. The catch tore the surface and I spent twenty minutes trying to recover it before admitting the piece was firewood.

By the third attempt, I was frustrated with myself on top of everything else I'd brought into the workshop. That frustration made my grip tighter, my movements more forced, my judgement more rushed. I was making decisions through irritation rather than observation. The wood wasn't cooperating and was not forgiving me for my disrespectful mood.

I finally stopped. Not because I'd figured anything out, but because I'd run out of patience. I stood there looking at the mess I'd made, time wasted, good timber ruined, deadline now tighter than ever, and I asked myself what had actually gone wrong.

The wood was fine. The tools were sharp. My technical skills hadn't evaporated overnight. What had gone wrong was that I'd never actually started the session properly. I'd begun working before I'd arrived. My hands were going through the motions while my mind was somewhere else, and the work suffered for it.

This is what I mean by finding your centre. Not the centre of the blank, though that matters too. I'm talking about *Your Centre.* The internal equilibrium that lets you be fully present with the work, responsive to what's actually happening rather than what happened earlier or might happen later.

The lathe is unforgiving in this regard. It doesn't care about your mood, your deadlines, your frustrations. It will only respond to what you're actually doing in the moment. If your attention is elsewhere, the work will show it. Not always dramatically, not always in catches and torn grain, but in subtle ways. Forms that lack conviction. Curves that don't quite flow. Decisions made from habit rather than intention. The tools seem to know when you're not really there.

What does it feel like when you are properly centred? For me, there's a settling that happens. The mental noise becomes quiet. I become aware of the workshop itself: the temperature, the light, the smell of wood and oil that lives in the space. My shoulders drop from where they've been creeping up toward my ears. My breathing slows and deepens without my having to think about it. I pick up the blank and actually feel it, its weight and balance, rather than just handling it mechanically.

In this state, I notice things I miss when I'm distracted. The subtle catch of grain that tells me to approach from a different angle. The slight imbalance that suggests the blank's true centre isn't quite where I marked it. The way the wood responds to each cut, the feedback through the tool that guides the next decision. All of this information is always there, but I can only properly receive it when I'm actually present.

The question, of course, is how to get there. How do you find your centre when life has knocked you off balance?

I've developed a simple ritual, nothing elaborate, just a few minutes of deliberate transition between whatever I was doing and the work ahead. I enter the workshop and I don't immediately start anything. I stand for a moment, looking around, checking my tools are where I want them. I have a cup of coffee and calm down. I notice where I am. Then I pick up the blank I'll be working with, turn it in my hands, feel its weight and texture. I'm not planning cuts yet, just making contact. Saying hello, if that doesn't sound too precious or too hippy.

This sequence takes perhaps two minutes. It changes everything about the session that follows. Without it, I could carry mental distraction into the work and spend the first hour trying to arrive while my hands are already busy. With it, I begin from a place of presence rather than fighting toward one.

The ritual doesn't have to be mine. What matters is having something that marks the transition, that creates a clear boundary between the noise of ordinary life and the focused attention the lathe demands. Some turners sharpen their tools before every session, not because the tools need it but because the rhythm of sharpening settles the mind (and also because it is a good idea, and freshly sharpened tools are a delight to use). Others tidy their workspace, clearing surfaces and organising tools as a way of clearing and organising their thoughts (I do this a lot). The specific practice matters less than the intention behind it: this is me arriving, this is me becoming present, this is me preparing to actually do the work rather than just going through the motions.

What happens when you skip this step? You probably know already. We've all had sessions where nothing went right, where the work felt like fighting, where pieces that should have been straightforward became inexplicably difficult. Sometimes, technical reasons account for this. Often, though, when I look back honestly at those sessions, the problem wasn't the wood or the tools or the techniques. The problem was that I never properly arrived. I started working while my mind was still elsewhere, and everything that followed was compromised by that divided attention.

When I notice these signs now, I stop. Not to berate myself for lacking focus, but to acknowledge that I haven't arrived yet and to give myself the chance to actually do so. Sometimes this means stepping back for a few minutes, making coffee, standing in the doorway and looking at the wonderful view out the back of the workshop, anything that breaks the momentum of distracted activity. Sometimes it means admitting that today isn't the day for it and choosing instead to do something mechanical, sanding or finishing or organising, that requires less presence than shaping new forms. A lot of the time, though, running my businesses takes me away from the lathe, and for too long.

There's no shame in this. The workshop will still be there when you're ready. The blank will wait. Forcing yourself to work when you're not present doesn't build discipline; it builds bad habits and produces poor work. It's better to acknowledge where you actually are and adjust accordingly.

I think of it as tuning an instrument before playing. A guitarist doesn't consider tuning to be separate from making music. It's part of the same process, the necessary preparation that makes good music possible. Finding your centre is tuning yourself. Bringing your attention and your body into alignment before asking them to work together on something that demands their cooperation.

There are days when this comes easily. You walk into the workshop already settled, already present, already eager to begin. Those are gift days. Enjoy them. But there are other days when the noise follows you through the door, when your mind refuses to let go of whatever you've been wrestling with, when presence feels like something you have to fight for.

On those days, be patient with yourself. The practice isn't about achieving perfect stillness. It's about recognising when you're not there yet and taking steps toward arriving. Even imperfect presence, attention that keeps wandering and needing to be brought back, is better than no attempt at presence at all. The returning is the practice.

I've come to value this preparation time as much as the turning itself. It's where I transition from one mode of being to another, from the scattered attention of daily life to the focused engagement that making requires. That transition doesn't happen automatically just because I've walked through a door. It needs to be cultivated, practiced, given space to occur.

The blank is patient. It will wait while you find your centre. What it won't do is compensate for your absence. The wood requires your full attention to reveal what it can become. Give it less than that and it will give you less in return.

So before you switch on the lathe, before you pick up the gouge, before you begin the work of shaping something from the raw material in front of you: check whether you've actually arrived. Take the time to find your centre. It's not a delay. It's where all good work begins.

3: What the Grain Remembers

BEFORE YOU CAN shape wood, you need to understand what wood is trying to tell you. Every blank has a history written in its grain. How it grew, where the light came from, which seasons were kind and which were harsh are all there. Learning to read that story is a skill a turner can develop, and one that takes years to refine.

I remember when I mounted a piece of spalted beech. The grain swirled like smoke, dark lines threading through pale cream, light pinks and greys. It was stunning, and I was excited to turn it. What I didn't yet understand was that all that beauty came with instructions. The spalting (the fungal decay that creates those dramatic patterns) had also made the wood fragile. It wanted to be cut gently, approached with patience, and finished with care. I discovered this the hard way, naturally, by pushing too hard and watching a beautiful section crumble.

The piece was on the lathe, I spun it up and after a few cuts, a third of it blew off and made extremely painful contact with my arm, leaving a nasty bruise there, and an even more bruised ego. Thankfully, no-one was there to see it.

That piece taught me to listen before I cut. The grain isn't decoration. It's information. It can tell you where the wood is strong, where it's weak, which direction will cut cleanly, and which will tear if you don’t approach it correctly. If you ignore it, the wood will remind you. If you work with it, the wood will cooperate in ways that feel almost generous.

There's a language to grain that you learn through experience. Straight grain, the kind you find in most timbers, is predictable. It cuts smoothly in both directions, holds detail well, and sands evenly. It's the wood equivalent of a steady student: reliable, consistent, maybe not the most exciting, but satisfying to work with. New turners often start here, and that's wise. You learn the fundamentals without the wood fighting back too hard.

Interlocked grain, common in species like elm or ash, is different. The fibres can spiral as they grow, creating a pattern that reverses direction every few growth rings. Cut one way and it's smooth. Cut the other and it tears. This wood teaches you about direction, about paying attention to how the tool responds. You can't zone out with interlocked grain. It demands presence.

The practical challenge with interlocked grain is that you'll often need to change your approach mid-cut. You might be getting beautiful ribbons of shaving, then suddenly the surface starts to tear and fuzz. That's the grain changing direction on you. The solution is perhaps to take much lighter passes through the difficult section. Some turners find that a shear scraping technique works well here, where you present the tool at a steep angle and essentially slice rather than cut. Sharp tools are essential. A dull edge that might cope with straight grain will make a mess of interlocked wood.

Wild grain, found in burrs (burls in the US), crotches, and sections where branches split or roots twist, is where things get interesting. This is chaos contained in wood form. The grain runs in multiple directions at once. Cut one area cleanly and you'll likely tear the next. These pieces require a different approach entirely: lighter cuts, sharp tools, constant attention, and possibly multiple tool directions to manage the shifting grain.

I've learnt to view wild grain as a conversation partner with strong opinions. It won't always accept whatever I propose. It has preferences, limitations, and a tendency to be dramatic when displeased. But when you find the right approach, when your tool angle, cutting direction, and pressure all align with what the wood can tolerate, the results are often more beautiful than anything you could have planned.

One exercise I use in teaching is to have students examine a blank before mounting it. Where does the grain run? Are there knots or defects? How dense does it feel? What the grain tells you about how the tree grew? Most people want to jump straight to turning, but this preliminary reading gives a moment of thought for the piece and how it may behave.

New makers choose with their eyes. Experienced makers choose with their hands, too. The prettiest blank isn't always the best blank for what you're trying to learn or create. Sometimes boring straight grain teaches you more than spectacular figured wood because it removes variables. You can focus on technique without the wood complicating things.

That said, there's something magical about working with challenging grain once you're ready for it. A piece of English walnut with its dark purple streaks, or olive ash with its wild patterns, or quarter-sawn oak with its medullary rays catching light. These woods have character that plain grain can't match. They're rewards for paying attention, for building the skills to work with complexity.

The grain also tells you about the wood's history. Wide growth rings indicate fast growth years, probably ample rainfall and nutrients. Tight rings suggest hardship: drought, competition, stress. Reaction wood, where the grain compresses on one side, shows where the tree was leaning or trying to correct its position. Sapwood versus heartwood tells you about age and function. All of this matters when you're turning because it affects how the wood will respond to your tools and how the finished piece will behave.

This is one of the things I love about woodturning that other crafts don't always offer: you're not working with a processed, uniform material. You're working with something that lived, responded to its environment, and carries memory in its structure. Every blank is unique, even within the same species, even from the same tree. Learning to read and respond to that uniqueness is part of the craft's depth[3].

The grain direction also determines finishing approaches. Wood with changing grain often needs different strategies: sanding with the lathe off (or (carefully) in reverse) to prevent fuzzing, using higher grit sequences, and applying a finish that can penetrate and stabilise the surface. Straight grain forgives more casual finishing. Wild grain demands respect even at the final stages.

There's also the question of movement. Wood isn't stable. It responds to humidity, expanding and contracting with seasonal changes[4]. Different grain orientations move differently. A bowl turned with the grain running rim-to-rim will distort differently from one turned with the grain running parallel to the axis. Neither is wrong, but understanding this helps you anticipate how a piece will behave after it leaves the lathe.

Some turners fight this. They want consistency, repeatability, and predictability. Those qualities are easier to achieve with man-made materials. Wood, by its nature, resists uniformity. That's either frustrating or freeing, depending on your perspective. I've come to see it as freeing. If I wanted every piece identical, I'd use a computer-controlled machine. I turn because I want collaboration with something more alive and random.

The grain also affects sound. This may seem minor, but auditory feedback during turning is crucial. Straight grain produces a consistent tone when cutting. Figured grain shifts in pitch as you work. Spalted or punky wood sounds different from dense heartwood. Experienced turners work with their eyes, ears, and hands.

I mention to students to listen for changes in the cutting sound. A smooth, consistent tone means clean cutting. The wood almost sings when everything is right: a steady, pleasant hum that tells you the fibres are separating cleanly. A lower pitch might indicate a dull tool struggling through the cut, or the grain becoming more difficult. A stuttering, interrupted sound suggests you're catching or the wood is punky and breaking rather than cutting. Sometimes you'll hear a crackling, almost like static, which often means you're tearing the grain rather than slicing it.

The lathe is like an instrument, and the grain determines what notes it can play. Learning to hear those notes is part of becoming proficient. I've caught myself sometimes listening more closely while making finishing cuts, letting my ears tell me what my eyes might miss. The sound changes before the surface shows damage, so if you're listening, you can adjust before you've created a problem.

There's also tactile feedback from grain. Dense, tight-grained wood feels solid under the tool. Loose, open-grained wood feels spongy[5]. Oily woods like rosewood or cocobolo feel slippery and leave residue on your tools. Resinous woods like pine are sticky. All of this information flows through the tool into your hands, teaching you what each wood needs.

I remember working with a piece of ancient bog oak once. It had been buried in peat for centuries and was almost black, incredibly hard, and unlike anything I'd worked with before. The grain was there but flaky through centuries of being wet and in the dark. Not exactly rotten, but relaxed and open, and very different to "normal" oak. My usual approaches didn't work. I had to slow down, take lighter cuts, keep the tool sharp, and essentially learn a new material. The grain was teaching me, but in a language I barely understood yet.

That experience reminded me that learning to read grain isn't something you finish. Every new species, every unusual piece, every unexpected characteristic is an opportunity to expand your vocabulary. You're building fluency in a language that has infinite dialects.

Sometimes the grain surprises you in pleasant ways. You'll be working along, expecting difficulty, and suddenly the wood cuts like butter. Or you'll hit a patch of figure you couldn't see before turning. A hidden curl pattern emerges as the surface becomes smooth. These moments feel like gifts, the wood revealing something it kept secret until you were ready to see it.

Other times, the surprises are less welcome. Hidden knots, internal cracks, bark inclusions, and insect damage (or even nails or, very rarely, bullets) are invisible from the outside, discovered only when cutting. This is where reading grain becomes prediction. Experienced turners develop an intuition about where problems might hide, based on external clues: bark patterns, weight distribution, and sound when tapped.

I occasionally tap blanks before mounting them, listening for hollow areas or internal voids. A solid blank produces a clear, resonant tone when you knock it with your knuckle. A blank with internal cracks or voids sounds duller, deader, sometimes with a slight rattle. It's not foolproof, but it gives you information. I also look at the bark carefully if it's still attached. Irregular bark patterns, unusual bulges, or areas where the bark seems loose can indicate problems underneath. And I feel the weight distribution, noting where the blank is denser or lighter than expected. A blank that feels surprisingly light in one area might have punky wood or hidden decay there.

None of this is certain. Wood is too variable for certainty.

But it reduces unpleasant surprises and helps you mount the blank in a way that avoids the worst areas or at least positions them where you can deal with them.

The relationship between grain and form is also worth considering. Some woods suit delicate, thin-walled forms because the grain runs consistently and holds detail. Others are better for robust, chunky pieces that don't stress the grain structure. A natural-edge bowl in figured maple can be striking because the figure provides visual interest while the form remains simple. The same form in plain beech might look boring. Matching grain character to form intention is part of design thinking.

The material isn't neutral. It has preferences and characteristics that should inform what you make. Fighting the wood's nature produces pieces that feel forced. Working with it creates pieces that feel inevitable, like the form was always hiding in the blank, waiting to be revealed.

I've been fortunate to work with wood from around the world. Australian burrs, African blackwood, South American exotic species. Each region's wood carries the character of its environment. Mediterranean olive is dense and tight-grained, reflecting dry climates. Pacific Northwest spalted maple is more chaotic, reflecting abundant moisture. The grain tells you where the wood lived before it came to your lathe.

This geographical storytelling adds layers to the work. When I turn a piece of English yew, I'm engaging with centuries of growth in a specific climate, with its own rainfall patterns, soil conditions, and sunlight. The grain carries all that history. Respecting that feels important to me, though I understand others might view it differently.

The grain also determines how light interacts with the finished piece. Straight grain reflects light evenly, creating a consistent appearance. Figured grain creates what's called chatoyance[6], a shimmering, three-dimensional effect where the appearance changes as you move. This is especially pronounced in woods like quilted maple or fiddleback ash. The grain isn't just structural. It's optical.

I've made many pieces from rippled sycamore that look almost holographic under changing light. The grain catches and reflects light differently from every angle, making the pieces seem to move even while stationary. That effect wasn't something I created. It was already in the wood. All I did was reveal it by cutting in a way that let the grain speak. Oh, and a decent amount of wood dye to accentuate the effect.

Over time, grain reading becomes intuitive. You don't consciously think, "This is interlocked grain, so I'll adjust my approach." You just feel the resistance, hear the change in tone, and your hands adapt. It's like learning a language. At first, you translate deliberately, but eventually, you think in the language itself. The grain speaks, and you understand without the intermediate step of interpretation.

I still study grain patterns, even after years of turning. New wood species, unusual growth patterns, and unexpected figure keep the work interesting. You can't master grain reading. You can only get better at it. That open-ended learning is one of the craft's great pleasures.

The grain connects you to biology, to ecology, to time. Every ring represents a year. Every pattern represents a response to conditions. The blank in your hands is a cross-section through history. Working with it isn't just craft. It's a form of reading, of translating growth into understanding[7].

I think this is why turning never becomes routine for me. Every piece of wood is something new to discover. Even if I'm making the same form repeatedly, the grain ensures each piece is unique. That variability keeps me engaged, keeps me learning, keeps the work alive. (If you know me, though, I'm not a production turner and turning many of the same pieces back-to-back bores me to tears!)

The grain speaks. The question is whether we're willing to listen. And like most worthwhile conversations, it rewards attention with insight, patience with beauty, and respect with cooperation. Learn to read the grain, and the wood teaches you to observe, to adapt, to work with nature rather than against it. These lessons extend far beyond the lathe.

4: The Extension of Self

YOUR TOOLS ARE an extension of your hands. The tool sits between your intention and the wood. If you can't trust the tool, you can't work freely. If the tool fights you, your attention splits between the wood and the implement. Trust in tools comes from four things: sharpness, familiarity, an honest assessment of what each tool can and cannot do and your skill level to use the tool correctly and safely.

I watch new students approach the tool rack with a mixture of reverence and confusion. So many options. So many shapes and names: roughing gouge, spindle gouge, bowl gouge, skew chisel, parting tool, scraper. Each has its purpose, its personality, its particular demands. The temptation is to think you need them all immediately. You don't. You only need a few tools you know intimately. The standard set of six tools will do 95% of any turning you're likely ever to do.

When I started turning, I had that standard set of tools. A spindle roughing gouge for taking spindle blanks to round. A spindle gouge for shaping. A parting tool for marking depths and parting off. A bowl gouge for hollowing and shaping. A round nose scraper for refining surfaces. And a skew chisel for the smoothest cuts possible. That was enough to make hundreds of pieces. More tools came later, as specific needs arose. But those six taught me everything fundamental about how steel meets wood.

The most important thing about any tool is not which one it is but whether it's sharp. A dull tool can be worse than no tool at all. It forces you to push harder, which creates catches. It tears the wood rather than cutting it. It makes you tentative when you should be confident. Every minute spent sharpening saves ten minutes of sanding and frustration. This isn't a theory. This is physics.

Sharpening is a skill in its own right[8], and one that takes time to develop. Early attempts will be inconsistent. You'll create facets when you want smooth bevels. You'll roll edges when you want crisp geometry. This is normal. The goal isn't perfection immediately but gradual improvement through repetition. Each time you sharpen, it teaches your hands something about pressure, angle, and motion.

I keep my sharpening system near my lathe. (It's a Robert Sorby ProEdge, if you're interested.) Not because I enjoy sharpening, but because accessible sharpening means I actually use it. If it's across the workshop, I'll delay sharpening too long. If it's within reach, I'll touch up an edge the moment I notice dulling. This small proximity makes an enormous difference to work quality.

There's a moment in every turning session when you realise the tool has dulled. The cut that was smooth becomes slightly rough. The chips that flew cleanly start to tear. Your body tenses slightly because the feedback has changed. You might not consciously register what's different at first, but something feels wrong. The tool that was gliding through the wood now seems to need pushing. The sound shifts from a clean whisper to something slightly harsher. The shavings change too: instead of long, consistent ribbons, you start getting shorter, more ragged pieces, or dust instead of chips.

This is the moment to stop and sharpen. The temptation is always to push on, to finish what you're doing before stopping. But continuing with a dull tool teaches your hands bad habits and produces poor surfaces. You compensate for the dullness by pushing harder, gripping tighter, adjusting your angle. All of these compensations become muscle memory if you do them often enough. Then when you finally sharpen and the tool cuts properly again, your technique has drifted and you readjust those compensations. It's far better to stop the moment you notice the change and restore the edge before bad habits form.

Tool handles matter more than people think. The wrong handle makes even a good tool uncomfortable to use. Too long and it becomes awkward. Too short and you lack leverage. Too thick and your hand cramps. Too thin and you can't grip securely. Handles are personal. What works for someone else might not work for you. This is why a few turners eventually make their own handles, fitting them precisely to hand size and preferred grip.

I've used different handles over the years. Each one teaches me something about ergonomics and preference. My current handles are a touch longer than standard length because I work a little further from the tool rest. They're a combination of aluminium and blackwood from a lovely company in Denmark. (Where they get them from is a secret I can't tease from them.) I love their weight and the fact that I can remove the blades and pack them up neatly for travelling to demonstrations. They also look fabulous, which I suppose makes me a "tool tart."

Trust also comes from understanding what each tool is meant to do. A roughing gouge excels at removing material quickly from spindle work, but can create a rough surface. It's designed for efficiency, not refinement. A spindle gouge can create delicate details but struggles with heavy cuts. Expecting it to rough out large blanks is unrealistic. Match the tool to the task. This seems obvious, but beginners often try to make one tool do everything or more often, use the wrong tool for the job, like using a *Spindle Roughing Gouge*[9] on a bowl. Most of the time, the job of the tool is its name and it can be very disappointing seeing and hearing the wrong tool for the job being used on social media.

The 3/8" bowl gouge (1/2" in the US) is probably the most

versatile tool in turning. With proper technique, it can rough, shape, and refine. It handles both inside and outside curves. It works across grain and with the grain. But even this workhorse has limits. It can't create fine details the way a spindle gouge can. It can't produce the crisp lines of a well-used skew. Knowing these limits prevents frustration. You aren't failing when a bowl gouge can't do detail work. You're just using the wrong tool.

Buy the best tools you can afford. Cheap steel holds an edge poorly, and a tool that fights you teaches bad habits. Three good tools will serve you better than ten poor ones.

Cheap tools often have handles that are too short, limiting control. They make learning harder rather than easier because you're fighting the tool as well as learning the technique.

That said, expensive tools don't make you a better turner. I've seen mediocre work produced with premium tools and excellent work made with basic implements. The tool is only as good as the skill directing it. Spending money on tools feels productive, but spending time practising with the tools you have is what actually improves work. Buy quality when you can afford it, but don't let tool acquisition substitute for tool mastery.

Familiarity breeds confidence (as well as contempt if you're not careful). A tool you've used hundreds of times behaves predictably. You know how much pressure it needs, what angle works best, and where it wants to grab. This knowledge sits in your hands and your head. You can't learn it from reading or watching. You learn it through use, through mistakes[10], through paying attention to how the tool responds to different approaches.

I can tell when someone picks up an unfamiliar tool. The grip is uncertain. The presentation angle shifts as they try to find what works. The cut is tentative. I remember the first time I tried a friend's bowl gouge that had a different grind than mine. Same basic tool, same general purpose, but the geometry was different enough that my usual approach didn't work. It took a minute or so of adjustment before I found how that particular tool wanted to be presented. My muscle memory was working against me because it was tuned to a different tool's geometry.

All of this is normal and necessary. Comfort comes from repetition. The first time you use any tool will feel awkward. The hundredth time will feel natural. The difference isn't the tool but the accumulated experience of using it.

There's also trust that comes from maintenance. Tools need care. They need cleaning after use, removing any resin and dust that accumulates. They need occasional attention to handles, checking for looseness or damage. Tightening ferrules, looking for cracks, and replacing when necessary. A tool that might fail mid-cut can't be trusted. A handle that might split under pressure creates anxiety that interferes with work. These small maintenance tasks are part of maintaining trust in your tools. You're ensuring they'll perform as needed when needed.

Trust in tools is ultimately trust in yourself. You've sharpened them properly. You've chosen the right tool for the task[11]. You know how this tool behaves and what it can do. You've practiced enough that your hands know what to expect. This confidence allows you to focus on the work rather than the implement. The tool disappears, becoming just an extension of intention. That's when real work happens.

Tool preference is personal and evolves with experience. Tools that felt perfect when I started feel wrong now because my technique has changed. My grip has evolved. My stance has shifted. What worked for earlier-me doesn't serve current-me the same way. This is normal. As you develop, your tools will evolve with you. Don't feel obligated to stick with something that no longer serves just because it once did.

There's also a social aspect to tools. Talking with other turners about tools, borrowing to try before buying, and seeing how others hold and use their implements creates shared knowledge. This accelerates learning beyond what solo exploration can achieve. No one has time to try every tool and every approach. Learning from others' experience saves much trial and error. But you still must find what works for you rather than blindly copying others.

Tool trust also affects workshop safety. A tool you trust allows relaxed vigilance, where you're alert but not anxious. A tool you distrust creates constant tension, which makes accidents more likely because it interferes with smooth movement and quick response. The safest work comes from trusting your properly maintained, familiar tools while remaining appropriately aware of their capabilities and risks.

So when I talk about trusting your tools, I'm talking about earned confidence through preparation, maintenance, practice, and honest assessment of capability. Build that foundation, and the tools become reliable partners. Neglect it and they become unreliable obstacles. The choice is yours, and the difference is everything.

5: The Edge of Everything

I CAN TELL you the exact moment I truly understood sharpening. Not when I learnt the technique, which came earlier. The moment of understanding came when I was teaching, watching a student struggle with a gouge that couldn't have cut warm butter, while I stood there with my mouth open trying to figure out how to say what I needed to say.

The problem with sharpening is that it's simultaneously the most important thing you'll learn in woodturning and the most difficult to teach. Not because the mechanics are complex, though there's nuance there, but because sharp is a feeling as much as it is a condition.

Let me start with something controversial: most beginners have no idea what sharp actually feels like. They think they do. They've seen sharp knives in their kitchen, sharp scissors cutting paper, sharp edges on broken glass. But a truly sharp woodturning tool, the kind of edge that can take whisper-thin shavings and leave a surface like silk, that's a different animal entirely.

This student I mentioned had been turning for about three months. Keen, diligent, watched all the right videos. Her gouge had what she called a "decent" edge. I watched her trying to shape a bowl, watched the tool push and bounce, watched the torn grain and bevel-rub marks accumulate, watched her frustration build.

I had a look at her tool, and it was what as I expected. An edge, certainly. A working edge, technically. But not a sharp edge. Not an edge that would cut cleanly but good enough to not be obviously dull, bad enough to make every cut a struggle.

I sharpened it properly. It took a few seconds on a new 180-grit belt on the ProEdge, and I handed it back to her. "Try now."

The change in her face and the quality of the cut was the moment I mentioned. That instant when someone experiences a well-sharpened tool for the first time. The tool that had been fighting her now glided through the wood like it was made of cream cheese. The bevel-rub stopped. The torn grain vanished. The wood sang instead of screamed.

And there it was. Her moment of understanding. The realisation that she'd been working harder than necessary, fighting her tools, blaming her technique, when the real problem was she simply didn't know how often to sharpen her tools, nor how to sharpen them effectively.

So let's establish what sharp actually means in woodturning. It means an edge refined to the point where the two surfaces (the bevel and the flute) meet at an angle sharp enough to slice wood fibres rather than push through them, tearing them.

But more practically, it means an edge that allows you to take the cut you want, at the thickness you want, with the control you need, leaving a surface that requires minimal sanding. Sharp is what makes everything else in woodturning possible.

The mechanics of sharpening are straightforward enough. You present your tool to an abrasive surface (a grinding wheel, for example, or an abrasive belt in my case) at the correct angle for that tool and move it across that surface until you've created a new edge. Keep going until you've achieved the level of sharp you're after.

Simple, right? Except that every part of that process contains layers of nuance that take time to master.

The angle, for instance. Too steep and your edge will be strong but won't cut cleanly. Too shallow and it'll cut beautifully for about thirty seconds before the edge fails. Every tool has an optimal angle, or rather, a range of optimal angles, depending on what you're cutting and how you're cutting it.

For bowl gouges, most turners settle on a range of 45 to 65 degrees. For spindle gouges, perhaps 35 to 45 degrees. For scrapers, often 60 to 80 degrees, sometimes with an additional bevel on top forming what's known as a "negative rake scraper." But these are starting points, not commandments. Your optimal angle might differ based on your technique, your lathe speed, the wood you're cutting, or the phase of the moon. Well, perhaps not that last one, but you take my point.

The key is consistency. If you sharpen at 60 degrees one day and 55 the next, you're not refining your edge but reshaping your tool. Every time you change the angle, you remove metal unnecessarily. Consistency means your tools stay the right shape and size for longer.

Every tool has an optimal angle range, and consistency matters more than hitting a precise number. I advocate for grinding jigs, particularly for beginners. A jig gives you consistency while you're learning what sharp feels like.

Later, when you've got that experience, when you can feel the difference between 55 and 60 degrees, when you know your tools intimately, then experiment with freehand if you want. But start with consistency. Give yourself that gift.

At the school, we use a Robert Sorby ProEdge with belts, and for wheel grinding, a 180-grit 8" CBN wheel alongside a white aluminium oxide wheel, dressed regularly and kept clean. The dressing is crucial. A glazed wheel is like trying to sharpen on glass. You need fresh, sharp abrasive particles exposed at the surface. The CBN wheel is a delight to use as it doesn't get smaller as it wears and doesn't need dressing, and it gives a superb edge. The belts on the ProEdge give me a super cutting edge, and the flat bevel I prefer over the hollow, concave bevel that wheels produce. We keep all these systems so we can demonstrate the use of each to students and explain the difference in them.

And use a light touch. I've seen beginners press their tools into the wheel as if they're trying to grind through to the other side. All you achieve is heat, burnt steel, and rapid wheel wear. Let the abrasive do the work. Present the tool, apply just enough pressure to maintain contact, and let the wheel cut.

The blue line? That telltale discolouration that appears when you've overheated your steel isn't a badge of enthusiasm. It's a sign you've just softened the edge you're trying to create. That section ideally needs grinding away, back to bright metal, before you can achieve proper sharpness. The blue indicates that the steel has lost its temper in that area, and temper is what allows it to hold an edge. You don't have to grind it away, using the edge will be fine, but you will sharpen more regularly whilst it naturally wears away.

Avoiding the blue line is mostly about patience and technique. Keep the tool moving across the wheel rather than holding it in one spot. Take lighter passes rather than trying to remove lots of metal at once. If you see colour starting to appear, stop immediately and let the tool cool before continuing. The few extra seconds this takes will save you grinding away damaged steel later.

For my finish cuts, for the last few passes on a bowl that will need minimal sanding, I want a nice new edge. It's a minute of work that saves possibly minutes of sanding, maybe more. And the surface it leaves is super. The difference between a good edge and a fresh edge is subtle but real, and for final cuts I believe it matters.

Even the best edge, sharpened to perfection, starts degrading the moment you touch wood with it. This is why sharpening isn't a thing you do occasionally. It's a rhythm you build into your work.

I sharpen often. Not because my edges fail dramatically. They don't. But because I can feel when they're no longer at their peak. The tool starts to push slightly rather than cut cleanly. The surface starts to need more effort. The wood stops singing.

These are subtle changes. Early on, you might not notice them. You might keep working with a degraded edge, wondering why things feel harder than they should. Experience teaches you to stop, refresh the edge, and continue. It takes thirty seconds. It transforms your next few cuts to get the job done.

This is the discipline that separates efficient turners from frustrated ones. Sharp tools make everything easier. Dull tools make everything a battle. It sounds obvious when I write it, but I've watched turners struggle through entire projects with edges that haven't been properly sharpened in days.

And there's the problem. Dull is a gradient, not a binary state. Your tools don't go from sharp to blunt in an instant. They degrade gradually, so gradually that you might not notice until you're well past the point where sharpening would have been wise.

I tell all my students that if they think their tool is dull, then they're too late!

This is why I advocate for what I call "preemptive sharpening." Don't wait until your tool is definitely dull. Sharpen when you feel the first hint of degradation, when the cut starts to require more effort, when the surface starts to look slightly less clean.

Build it into your workflow. Here's what this looks like in practice: I'm roughing out a bowl, removing the bulk waste, getting the basic shape established. That's hard work for the tool, lots of material coming off quickly. When the roughing is done, before I start refining, I sharpen. It takes thirty seconds. Then I refine the outside curve, working towards the final shape. Before I flip to hollow the inside, I sharpen again. Another thirty seconds. I hollow, taking care with the end grain sections. Before my final finishing passes, one more sharpen. By the time the bowl is done, I might have sharpened three or four times. Total time at the grinder: maybe two minutes. Time saved in sanding and frustration: considerably more than two minutes.

This rhythm becomes automatic. You stop thinking of sharpening as an interruption and start thinking of it as a natural pause in the work, like taking a breath between sentences. It's not slowing you down. It's keeping everything flowing smoothly.

There's also the question of what to sharpen. I meet turners who'll spend ages perfecting their bowl gouges while their scrapers remain neglected, their skews gathering dust with edges that wouldn't cut butter. Every tool in your rack deserves the same attention.

A scraper with a proper edge is a revelation if you've only ever used dull ones. The difference is dramatic. A dull scraper pushes and chatters, leaving a surface that needs extensive sanding. A sharp scraper, with a fresh burr raised on the edge, slices cleanly and can leave a surface nearly ready for finish. The transformation when you first use a properly sharpened scraper is almost as dramatic as my student's experience with her gouge. Suddenly a tool you thought was limited becomes genuinely useful.

A sharp skew makes planing cuts that leave surfaces requiring minimal sanding. The skew has a reputation for being difficult, and much of that reputation comes from people trying to use dull ones. A sharp skew, properly presented, produces the cleanest cut in woodturning. A dull skew catches, digs, and generally misbehaves in ways that make it seem like a dangerous tool. It's not the tool that's the problem.

Even your parting tool, perhaps especially your parting tool, transforms when properly sharp. A dull parting tool burns and binds, generating heat and friction that can scorch the wood and make the cut feel dangerous. A sharp one cuts cleanly and quickly, with no burning, no binding, just clean separation.

Give every tool equal attention. This might seem like extra work. It isn't. It's investing minutes to save hours. It's respecting your tools and, by extension, respecting your work and yourself.

The student I mentioned learnt this. I showed her how to sharpen her gouge, but more importantly, I showed her what sharp felt like. She took that knowledge, practiced it, and made it part of her routine.

That's the goal. Not just the ability to sharpen, but the awareness of when sharpening is needed, the discipline to do it promptly, and the understanding that this isn't peripheral to woodturning but absolutely central.

Because here's the truth they don't emphasise enough: no amount of technique compensates for a dull tool. You can have perfect stance, perfect tool control, perfect understanding of grain and cut direction. But if your edge isn't sharp, you'll struggle. You'll catch. You'll tear. You'll wonder why something that looks so easy when others do it feels so difficult for you.

The answer is often brutally simple: their tools are sharp. Yours aren't. Not properly. Not yet.

So learn to sharpen. The mechanics are straightforward. Learn the feel of it. Learn what sharp is, what it sounds like, and what it enables. Build it into your practice as fundamental, not optional. Maintain it as routine, not intervention.

Your tools are the interface between your intention and the wood. Keep them sharp, and that interface becomes transparent, allowing your skills to flow freely. Let them dull, and everything becomes harder than it needs to be.

It's a simple lesson. Perhaps too simple. But simple doesn't mean unimportant. Sometimes the most fundamental lessons are the ones that make everything else possible.

Sharpen your tools. Sharpen them well. Sharpen them often. Everything else follows from this.

6: The Space Between Cuts

THERE'S A RHYTHM to woodturning that turners rarely notice at first. They're too focused on the cuts themselves: where the tool enters the wood, the shavings flying, the shape emerging. What they miss, what takes time to see, is that the cuts are only half the story.

The other half is the part that separates frantic work from controlled craft. It lives in the space between the cuts.

I had a student once who turned like he was trying to win a race against time itself. The tool hitting the wood, shavings flying, the tool moving quickly and barely pausing for breath. His pieces emerged quickly. They also emerged poorly. Lumpy, uneven, with catches and digs that betrayed his haste.

"Slow down," I suggested after watching this frenzied display.

He looked at me like I'd suggested he work with blunt tools. "But I want to get better faster," he said, which might be the most wonderfully ironic statement I'd ever heard.

So I showed him something different. I brought my gouge to his piece, made a cut. Then stopped. Looked at what I'd just done. Assessed the surface, the wall thickness, and the shape development. Made another cut. Stopped again. Repeated this pattern: cut, observe, cut, observe, until the piece was complete.

"That took you the same time as my way," he observed.

"Look at the results," I said.

He did. My piece was smooth, even, well-proportioned. His looked pitted, marked, faceted and torn. It took the same amount of time but with vastly different outcomes. The difference wasn't in the cutting. It was in the spaces between.

This is one of those lessons that seems almost too simple to be important. Pausing between cuts. How hard can it be? But like most simple things in woodturning, the depth reveals itself slowly.

When you pause between cuts, you're not just resting. You're observing. You're reading the piece, understanding how it's responding to your work, seeing where you need to remove more material, where you need to refine, where the shape is developing well and where it needs adjustment.

What does this observation actually look like? You're checking whether your curve is flowing smoothly or whether there's a flat spot developing. You're looking at the wall thickness if you're hollowing, watching for areas that are getting thin too quickly or staying too thick. You're reading the surface quality, noticing where the cut was clean and where it started to tear. You're feeling with your fingers for ridges or bumps that your eyes might miss. All of this information shapes your next cut.

You're also letting the wood settle. Each cut creates stresses in the material, causes slight flexing, generates heat. These effects need a little time to dissipate. Rush from one cut to the next without a pause, and you're working with a piece that's constantly in motion, constantly reacting to your last intervention.

That's like trying to aim at a target while the target is still wobbling from your last shot. Possible, certainly. But why make it harder than it needs to be?

The pause also gives you time to plan your next cut. Where will the tool enter? At what angle? With what depth? These decisions, made in the moment with observation informing your choice, are far more accurate than decisions made in a rushed blur of continuous cutting.

Think about it this way: when you're driving somewhere

unfamiliar, you occasionally check your map or GPS. You don't just point the car in a vague direction and hope for the best. You check, adjust, check again. Turning without pausing to observe is like driving with your eyes closed between junctions, which is extreme and definitely not recommended!

But there's more to these pauses than practical observation. There's something almost meditative about the rhythm of cut[12] and pause, work and assessment. It creates a breathing space in the work, a cadence that keeps you present and aware.

I find my best work happens in this rhythm. Not when I'm pushing hard, not when I'm in a rush, but when I'm allowing each cut to inform the next[13], when I'm giving myself permission to pause and think.

My student learnt this, eventually. He fought it at first. His instinct was always to keep moving, to fill every second with activity, to get better faster. But after an hour or so of forced pausing, of making himself stop and look between cuts, something shifted.

"I'm working more slowly", he said, "but I'm making progress faster. How does that work?"

"Because you're not fixing mistakes," I pointed out. "You're not removing catches, not correcting lumps, not trying to salvage what your rushing created. You're just making it right the first time."

That's the efficiency of the pause. It feels slower. It *is* slower in the moment. But it's faster overall because you're not creating problems that need fixing. You're observing, adjusting, and working with what's actually there rather than what you think is there.

There's also a safety element here that doesn't get discussed enough. When you're pausing regularly, when you're stepping back to observe, you're naturally giving yourself recovery time if something goes wrong. Your tool is out of the cut, your body is slightly more relaxed, your mind is clear rather than tunnel-visioned on continuous action.

I've seen catches happen during extended periods of continuous cutting. The turner enters a flow state, which appears positive but can be dangerous. They stop seeing clearly, stop reacting to small signs of trouble, keep pushing through when they should stop and reassess.

I remember watching a video of someone working on a natural-edge bowl, cutting continuously, almost hypnotically. In a paused, observational state, he'd have noticed the bark was coming off. In his continuous cutting trance, he didn't. The bark section released, the tool caught the exposed edge of the piece, and it came off the lathe. No injury, fortunately, but a ruined piece and a shaken content creator. Had he been pausing and observing, I believe he'd have seen the bark lifting and either stabilised it or adjusted his approach.

The pause breaks this hypnotic state. It returns you to awareness, to conscious control[14]. It's a reset button that you press regularly, keeping yourself attentive rather than automatic and vulnerable.

Now, I should clarify what I mean by "pause." I'm not suggesting you stop for minutes at a time between each cut. That would be ridiculous. The pause I'm advocating is brief. Perhaps only a few seconds, sometimes less. Just long enough to pull back, look, assess, and plan. The pauses become shorter with experience as your observation becomes more efficient and your decisions more intuitive.

It's the difference between continuous motion and controlled motion. Between working in a blur and working with intention. Between hoping for good results and creating them deliberately.

An extra ten seconds of observation might save you a minute or two of sanding. That's not just efficient. It's transformative to your workflow.

There's also something to be said for the psychological benefit of the pause. Turning can be intense, focused work. Your body is engaged, your mind is tracking multiple variables, your eyes are monitoring tool position and surface quality and a dozen other factors.

Without regular breaks, even brief ones, fatigue accumulates faster than you realise. Your shoulders tense, creeping up toward your ears without you noticing. Your grip tightens on the tool handle until your forearm starts to ache. Your breathing shallows, and you might even hold your breath during difficult cuts without realising it. Your stance shifts as tired legs compensate, and suddenly your tool presentation angle has changed and you don't know why your cuts feel different.

These physical changes affect your turning, usually in subtle ways you don't immediately notice. But they accumulate. By the end of an hour of continuous cutting, you're not the same turner you were at the start. You're tighter, more fatigued, less precise.

The pause gives you a moment to reset physically as well as mentally. Breathe. Relax your shoulders. Loosen your grip. Reset your stance. These micro-adjustments prevent the fatigue that leads to poor decisions and inconsistent cuts. Each pause is a small reset that keeps you fresh throughout the session.

I've found that turners who pause regularly can work longer sessions with better results than those who push through continuously. It's counterintuitive, perhaps. You'd think continuous work would be more productive. But the human body and mind don't work that way. We need rhythm, we need variation, we need these small moments of recovery.

My student's pieces improved dramatically. More than that, he enjoyed the work more. The frantic energy that had characterised his early turning, his sense of fighting the wood, transformed into something calmer. Not passive, but measured. Not slow, but controlled.

This is what I want you to understand about the space between cuts: it's not dead time. It's not wasted motion. It's an essential part of the work, as important as the cutting itself.

In these spaces, you read the wood. You assess your progress. You plan your next moves. You reset your body and mind. You maintain the clarity and focus that good turning demands.

Without these spaces, you're just removing wood. With them, you're crafting something with intention and awareness.

So slow down. Not in the way that suggests timidity or uncertainty. Slow down in a way that allows observation, that creates space for conscious choice, that keeps you present and aware throughout the work[15].

Cut, pause, observe. Cut, pause, observe. Let this become your rhythm. Let it feel natural rather than forced. Let it transform your turning from frantic activity into measured craft.

Your pieces will show the difference. You'll notice a difference in your confidence, in your control, and in your relationship with the wood and the process.

The space between cuts is where good turning happens, in the thoughtful rhythm of work and observation, action and assessment.

Learn to value these spaces. Learn to use them. Learn to trust that the pause isn't interrupting your work. It's helping to enable it.

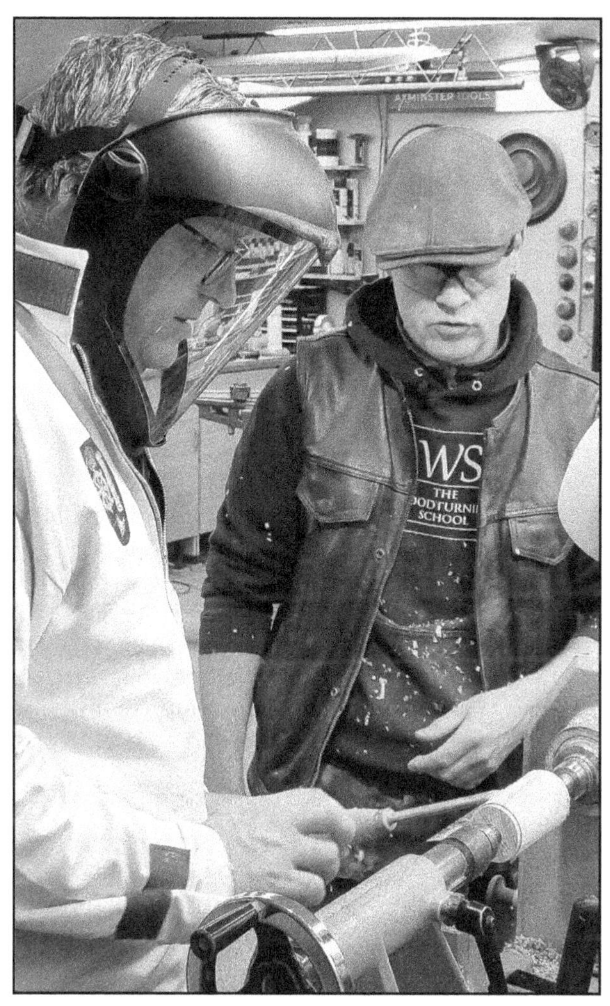

Sometime in 2024, a student learns about the bevel of the tool.

Part Two

What the Mind Sees

Once the hands have their basic vocabulary, the mind begins to shape what they do. This chapter explores how we think about the work: how feeling guides form, why patience carries weight, what accidents and recoveries teach us, how wood communicates if we're listening, and where the boundaries of our craft actually lie. The mind doesn't replace the hands. It works alongside them, bringing intention and understanding to what would otherwise be mere movement.

7: Form Follows Feeling

THERE'S A MOMENT in every turner's development, if they're lucky and if they stick with it long enough, when something shifts. The piece on the lathe stops being an exercise in technique and becomes something more. A conversation, perhaps.

I remember my moment clearly. I'd been turning for perhaps three years, was technically competent, could produce consistent work. But everything I made looked safe. Cautious. I was so focused on avoiding mistakes that I'd forgotten to invite possibility.

Then one day, while working on a bowl, I consciously chose to follow the golden ratio more deliberately than I ever had before[16]. Not as a rulebook requirement, but as an exploration. I stopped, looked at what was emerging, and thought: "Yes. This is what happens when you trust the principles rather than fear them."

What emerged was the first piece I'd made that felt alive (in a funny sort of way). It had personality. It had feeling.[17] The proportions weren't accidental. They were intentional in a way my previous work had been cautious.

This is what I mean by "form follows feeling." Not that technique doesn't matter, because it absolutely does. Not that understanding proportion and design principles isn't important, because it's crucial. But there comes a point where you stop treating the rules as constraints and start experiencing them as possibilities.

I see this progression in many turners, particularly those who come to the craft with strong academic or technical backgrounds. They arrive with an understanding of design theory, can discuss the golden ratio and the rule of thirds. Their early pieces are often textbook examples of good design. Well-proportioned. Correctly executed. And yet somehow tentative.

You can see it in their work. The proportions are right, but they feel calculated rather than felt. The curves are smooth, but they don't flow with confidence. There's a quality of careful measurement in every line, as if the piece is constantly checking itself against a standard rather than simply being what it wants to be. These aren't bad pieces. They're often quite accomplished technically. But they have a hesitancy that holds them back from being truly compelling.

The shift happens when they begin to trust what they know. When they stop treating principles as tests to pass and start experiencing them as foundations to build upon. When they realise that understanding the golden ratio means you can explore with it, play with it, let it inform your choices rather than dictate them.

This isn't about abandoning measurement or ignoring design principles. It's about internalising them so completely that they become instinctive rather than a checklist. It's moving from "does this match the golden ratio?" to "does this feel harmonious?" and trusting that your educated eye can tell the difference.

There comes a point where the measurements and calculations inform something more intuitive. You look at the piece on the lathe, at the form developing, and you know with logical certainty that it's working[18]. Or that it needs adjustment. Or that it's inviting you toward something you hadn't initially imagined.

This knowing isn't mystical, though it can feel that way when you're new to trusting it. It's accumulated experience with plenty of observations turned into instinct. It's your brain processing proportions and curves and relationships faster than conscious thought, then presenting you with a feeling of rightness or possibility.

The challenge is learning to trust it, especially if you come from a background that values measurable correctness, particularly if you've been conditioned to treat rules as tests rather than tools for exploration.

But here's what I've learnt: the principles (like the golden ratio and the rule of thirds) are foundations, not ceilings. They're essential when you're learning, giving you frameworks and reference points. But at some stage, if you want to develop your own voice, your own style, your own relationship with the work, you need to build upward from that foundation with confidence.

This doesn't mean ignoring everything you know. A piece that disregards every principle of good design isn't automatically interesting just because it's experimental. But a piece that explores principles with genuine curiosity and confidence often has a quality that cautious correctness can't achieve.

The sweet spot (and it's very sweet when you find it) is when your technical knowledge empowers your intuition rather than limiting it. When you understand the golden ratio, the rule of thirds, or other design principles well enough that you can feel when a proportion is harmonious without measuring it[19]. When you grasp balance and weight distribution so thoroughly that your eye automatically recognises when something is working.

Here's what this looks like in practice. You're shaping a bowl, and you've roughed out the basic form. According to your original sketch, the rim should be at a certain diameter, the curve should follow a particular arc. But as you refine, something feels off. The form wants to be slightly taller, slightly narrower. You don't measure this. You feel it. And because you've internalised the principles, you know this adjustment will actually improve the proportions rather than break them. You follow the feeling, and what emerges is better than what you planned.

Eventually, the checking, measuring, and verification become a final check rather than a constant companion. The turner knows the wall is right before they measure. The measurement just confirms what their hands already told them. This is internalised expertise, and it applies to proportion and form just as much as it applies to wall thickness.

This is what "form follows feeling" means in practice. It means having the technical foundation to make informed choices, then having the confidence to let feeling guide how you apply those choices. It means trusting that the piece developing on the lathe can teach you something about what's possible.

This responsive approach requires confidence, which is why it tends to develop as a turner's journey progresses. Early on, you benefit from the certainty of plans and measurements. Knowing that if you follow these steps, you'll get these results builds skills and confidence.

But there comes a stage where you're ready for more. Following the plan exactly might mean missing opportunities, overlooking what the wood is offering, and creating pieces that are technically accomplished but less expressive than they could be.

The transition from following rules to exploring with them is a gradual awakening. I've watched turners navigate it, sometimes uncertain about the apparent openness of "trust your feeling," wanting clearer guidance.

But I can't make this clearer in the way rules are clear because it's learnt through making pieces that surprise you. Through gradually developing the eye and the confidence to trust what you see and feel.

The principles remain useful because they inform your eye, guide your initial decisions, and provide a foundation as you explore. But they stop limiting every choice. They become one voice among several, and increasingly, your own voice is the one you trust most.

This is what I want you to understand: the technical foundation matters enormously. Learn the proportions. Study good design. Understand why certain forms work and others don't. This knowledge is essential.

But don't stop there. Don't let the principles become limits on what you explore. As your skills develop, as your eye becomes more educated, start trusting your responses. Start allowing feeling to inform how you apply form. Start listening to what emerges rather than just imposing what you planned.

This is moving from external rules to internalised experience. It's developing the confidence to make choices based on accumulated knowledge rather than conscious calculation alone.

The pieces that emerge from this approach, when it works (and it works increasingly often), have something special. They feel intentional and alive, considered but not overthought. They have the quality of having been discovered and made, both at once.

This is what I'm encouraging you toward. Not recklessness, not abandoning everything you've learnt. But the confidence to let feeling inform how you apply form, to trust your developing expertise, to follow where the work leads even when it takes you somewhere unexpected.

Form follows feeling. Not immediately, not without foundation. But gradually, as you develop the skills and the confidence to allow it.

That's when your work stops being an exercise in proving competence and becomes an expression of something more profound with the craft, and with yourself.

Trust the principles while you're learning them. Then let feeling guide how you apply them, and see what emerges.

8: The Weight of Patience

PATIENCE ISN'T PARTICULARLY fashionable in modern life. We value speed, efficiency, and getting things done quickly. We have fast food, fast fashion, fast everything. The idea of deliberately working slowly, of taking time when you could rush, of choosing the patient approach over the expedient one feels almost transgressive.

Woodturning doesn't care about modern sensibilities. It demands patience whether you want to give it or not. Try to rush, try to force the process, and the wood will teach you (occasionally painfully) that some things simply cannot be hurried[20].

I learnt this lesson quite early. I wish I could say I learnt it gracefully, but I was younger, eager, and convinced that with enough enthusiasm, I could overcome any obstacle. I'd been turning for about sixteen months and was starting to feel confident. I'd even sold a few pieces.

Going into October, I thought it would be a good time to start making some Christmas trees for sale in the coming months. I was on my third or fourth of the day, and I'd filmed a couple of them as "B Roll" for a YouTube video series I was filming at the time called Turner's Journey.

So there I was with the fourth piece of freshly cut Leylandii branch mounted up between centres and with spindle roughing gouge in hand, went at it with lots of confidence, and dare I say, a bit of complacency, too. I was getting bored with turning the same thing. You already know I don't like repetitive turning, but there I was on the fourth Christmas Tree of the day.

If you're wincing already, you know how this ended. And

if you're one of my students, you'll definitely know this story.

I didn't even get one cut finished when the piece was ripped from the centres, ricocheting off my (inexpensive) face shield, leaving me with a bloodied and broken nose, two black eyes, and severely bruised confidence.

In my rush to get that blasted tree turned, I didn't even look over the branch to check for knots or the stubby bits of twigs I'd removed prior to turning. I'd rushed what shouldn't have been rushed, choosing impatience over process, and was told, in no uncertain and painful terms by the wood and the machine, that patience isn't optional in this craft. It's fundamental. And the weight of impatience, the cost of trying to force things to happen faster than they should, is almost always heavier than the burden of waiting.

This lesson applies to every aspect of woodturning, though it manifests differently depending on what you're doing.

Take tool preparation, for example. A properly sharpened edge doesn't happen in five seconds. It takes time to work the bevel to that edge just so. Rush it, and you end up with an edge that looks sharp but fails quickly, that tears rather than cuts, that makes every subsequent operation harder than it needs to be.

The same applies to mounting work. Taking time to find the right centre, to ensure your blank is secure, to check alignment. This might add two minutes to your setup. But it saves the frustration of working with a piece that wobbles, or catches, or flies off the lathe (as I found out) because you couldn't be bothered to mount it or present the tool properly.

The actual turning process demands perhaps the most obvious patience. Light cuts, working systematically, reading the wood as you go. These take time. You can work faster, certainly. Take too heavy a cut, push your tools harder, skip the checking and measuring and things may come a cropper.

You'll finish more quickly. You may also end up with more catches, more torn grain, and more design compromises because you removed too much material and couldn't go back. The speed savings evaporate when you factor in the fixing time, or worse, when you realise the piece is beyond fixing and needs to be scrapped.

What should take five minutes takes fifteen, because you keep having to go back to coarser grits to remove scratches you should have dealt with earlier. Or worse, you apply the finish and discover all those scratches you thought were gone are suddenly visible, highlighted by dyes, oil or lacquer.

Patience in sanding means working through each grit thoroughly before progressing. It means spending the time at 120 grit until every tool mark is gone before you even think about 180. It means checking the surface under good light, running your fingers across it, looking for the scratches that hide in the grain. It means accepting that jumping from 120 to 400 because you're bored doesn't actually save time. It just delays the discovery that you needed to do the work properly.

I tell students they're not just smoothing the surface. They're removing the scratch pattern left by the coarser grit and replacing it with a finer one. If you don't fully remove that coarser pattern, it's still there under the finer scratches, waiting to reveal itself when you apply the finish. Patient sanding isn't about going slowly. It's about being thorough at each stage before moving on.

But perhaps the most demanding patience comes in wood preparation and drying. This is measured not in minutes or hours but in weeks or months. And for beginners, especially for people conditioned to instant gratification, this timeline can feel almost insulting.

You find a beautiful piece of wood. You want to turn it now. But it's wet, or not quite dry enough, or needs sealing and time before it's ready. You could try to work with it anyway, and sometimes people get lucky in a process called *rough turning*. Quite often though, they end up with a split piece and a lesson in patience they didn't want to learn.

One great solution is having multiple projects at different stages. While one piece is drying, you're working on others. While one item is being glued and needs to cure, you're preparing something else. This layering of projects means you're always working, but you're also always allowing adequate time for each stage.

Here's what this looks like in practice. On any given day, you might have three or four bowls rough-turned and drying on a shelf (or dozens in the case of production turners), waiting for the moisture content to stabilise. I might have a couple of blanks sealed and resting, not yet ready to mount. I might have one piece on the lathe being finished, and another waiting for its final coat of finish to cure. None of these projects is being rushed. All of them are progressing at their proper pace. But I'm never standing idle waiting for one piece to be ready. There's always something at the right stage for work.

It's a different kind of productivity. Not the sprint of continuous work on one piece, but the sustainable pace of managing multiple pieces through their various stages. Less exciting perhaps, but far more effective. Though it could be more exciting, as you can be working on a vase one day, a box the next, and a nest of bowls the one after that.

This is what patience in woodturning looks like. Not passive waiting, not doing nothing. But active patience. Making progress at the pace the work demands, accepting that some stages cannot be rushed, trusting that the time invested in doing things properly pays dividends in the final result.

I feel I ought to share my own current experience of patience before continuing. With the amount of time administering the school takes, I must be patient before I can turn again and work on new projects for my next book, or video, or even just turning for *me.* It's frustrating, but necessary to keep earning a living!

But the wood doesn't care about this conditioning. The lathe doesn't reward haste. The piece you're making will be what it will be based on the care and time you give it, not on how quickly you want to finish.

So learn patience. Not because it's virtuous (though perhaps it is) but because it's practical. Because impatient work is almost always worse work. Because the weight of fixing rushed mistakes is heavier than the burden of working carefully from the start.

Take the time to sharpen properly. Mount your work carefully. Make controlled cuts. Sand through each grit thoroughly. Allow wood to dry at its own pace (even in a kiln). Work on multiple pieces so you're always productive but never rushing.

These practices might feel slow at first. They might seem inefficient compared with the rush of continuous, rapid work. But they're sustainable and effective.

And perhaps most importantly, they allow you to be present with your work rather than constantly ahead of it, mentally rushing toward completion while your tools are still shaping the piece.

Patience is a weight, certainly. It can feel heavy, especially when you're eager to see results, to finish, to move on to the next thing. But it's a different kind of weight than the burden of rushed work, of mistakes made in haste, of pieces ruined because you couldn't wait.

Learn to carry this weight. Let it slow you down, yes, but in the way that makes everything better rather than just taking longer. Let it teach you to work with the craft's natural pace rather than fighting it.

The pieces that emerge from patient work have a quality that rushed work never achieves. They feel considered, careful, complete. They reflect the time invested in them, and that reflection is beautiful.

So slow down. Not because speed is wrong, but because the right pace varies and often requires more patience than you initially want to give. Trust that the time is worth it. Trust that patience, though it carries weight, is lighter than the alternative.

9: Happy Accidents

ON THE WALL in the school is a quarter of the piece that came off the lathe I talked about in the last lesson. It's mounted to a plaque with a pyrographed caption that reads:

"The Catch That Tried to Break My Nose, 15th October 2015"

For me, it's important to have it there. It serves as a reminder that accidents can happen if you don't have respect for the machine, the tools and wood, and it's a good anecdote for the health and safety briefing that all students go through before the start of a lesson.

You'll remember in the last lesson that I said it broke my nose, but the caption above says that it tried to break my nose. Well, it still hurt at Christmas that year, so I'm pretty sure it was broken. Lesson learnt (but thankfully my nose healed straight).

This approach to learning from accidents rather than hiding from them isn't particularly intuitive. We're taught to avoid mistakes, to treat failure as something shameful, to aim for perfection from the start. But real life has no room for this kind of thinking. Accidents will happen. The only question is whether you'll learn from them.

Let me start with catches, because if you're going to have accidents in woodturning, catches are your most frequent teacher. A catch is when your tool, instead of cutting smoothly, suddenly digs into the wood and gets yanked from your control. It's violent. It's loud. And the first few times it happens, it can be terrifying.

My first serious catch was the one on the Christmas tree. The spindle roughing gouge grabbed a knot in the wood on the tailstock end, dug in, and the piece was ripped from the lathe, straight into my face shield. It all happened so quickly, yet the piece came towards me very slowly. I remember it incredibly clearly.

That was the accident. The learning came afterwards, when I stopped shaking, cleaned myself up and started being curious. What had I done wrong? Why had the tool grabbed at that particular moment? What could I do differently to prevent it from happening again?

I examined the catch mark, looked at where my tool had been, and replayed the moment in my mind. And I started to understand: I hadn't checked over the piece for knots or other features that should have been noted. As a permanent reminder, I took it, cut it down and mounted it to the plaque that now hangs in the school. I can't say it hangs proudly as I should have known better. But as I said, it's a suitable anecdote to share during a health and safety briefing.

That single accident taught me more about patience and preparation than anything else. When everything works smoothly, you don't need to know why. When things go wrong, you're forced to understand. The lesson is burned in by adrenaline and frustration, occasionally a good amount of pain, and the very real desire to never have that happen again.

This is the pattern with accidents: they're uncomfortable but remarkably effective teachers.

On a slightly softer note, but no less frustrating, take cutting through to the bottom of a bowl. Many turners refer to this as turning a funnel, or joining the *Funnel Club*. It's an accident most turners have at some point. You're refining the internal curve, taking light cuts, checking thickness with your fingers. Then suddenly there's daylight where there shouldn't be any, and you've dropped through the bottom. (This is most common when turning with a recess mounting method.) You've gone too far, removed too much material, and now you have a bowl with a viewing window. In other words, a funnel. Or a lamp shade.

The accident is frustrating. The learning is valuable. You discover exactly how thin is too thin. You learn what it feels like when you're approaching the danger zone, that slightly different vibration through the tool, that change in sound as the wall gets thinner. You develop a better sense of wall thickness and how it varies around the bowl, particularly how the base can sneak up on you when you're focused on the walls.

After my first funnel, I started being much more deliberate about checking thickness at the centre, not just around the sides. I learnt to feel for that moment when the wood starts to flex slightly because there's not enough material behind it. These weren't things I could have learnt easily from a book or video. They came from the visceral experience of suddenly seeing light where wood should have been.

Next time, you'll be more careful because you'll understand the limits better. That understanding, which no amount of careful work could have taught you, came from the accident.

Or consider the accident of removing too much material from a design element. You're working on a detail, some decorative element, and you get carried away. Or you're chasing a shape that's running away from you. The detail intended to be prominent becomes subtle. The feature you wanted to emphasise disappears entirely.

Frustrating? Certainly. But you learn about proportion, about how much detail you need to leave for it to register visually, about the difference between your close-up view and what others will see from a normal distance. These lessons stick because they cost something. The cost is the piece you were making, and that investment embeds the knowledge.

There's also the category of happy accidents, those mistakes that turn into features. I've had catches create interesting texture in a surface I was planning to keep smooth. I've had splits develop into decorative elements when filled with coffee grounds or metal powders[21]. I've had proportions go wrong in ways that turned out more interesting than my original plan.

Let me tell you about one of these recoveries. I was working on a small bowl that developed a crack during drying. Not a dramatic split, but enough to ruin the piece if I left it as was. Rather than scrap it, I decided to experiment. I mixed fine coffee grounds with CA glue and worked the mixture into the crack, then sanded it back once cured[22]. What emerged was a dark line that looked almost like natural figure in the wood. It wasn't what I'd planned, but it was genuinely interesting. That accident taught me a technique I've used deliberately many times since.

The skill here is recognising when an accident offers an opportunity. Not every mistake can be salvaged, and not every attempt to turn an accident into an intentional feature works. But sometimes the result is enough to make it worth paying attention. An accident can sometimes show you a better direction than the one you were heading in.

This is the more profound lesson about accidents[23]: they're not just teaching moments about what went wrong. They're also opportunities to discover what might go right in unexpected ways. They force you out of your planned approach and into improvisation. Sometimes that improvisation reveals better solutions than your original plan.

But all this requires a particular mindset. You have to be willing to see accidents as information rather than failure. You have to be curious about what went wrong rather than just frustrated. You have to be open to unexpected directions rather than rigidly attached to your original vision.

There's an important distinction to make here: accidents that come from pushing boundaries versus accidents that come from carelessness. You learn from both, certainly. But one type teaches you about the craft's limits. The other type teaches you about your own limits of focus and discipline. Both lessons are valuable, and ought to be learnt by every turner, consciously or not.

Consider the difference. A turner experimenting with how thin they can take a bowl wall, pushing gradually thinner with each piece, eventually goes too far and creates a hole. That's a boundary-pushing accident. They've learnt exactly where the limit is for that species, that wall angle, that tool approach. Valuable information that will inform every thin-walled piece they make afterwards.

Now consider a turner who goes through the bottom of a bowl because they were thinking about dinner, or rushing to finish before an appointment, or simply not paying attention to what their hands were doing. That's a carelessness accident. They haven't learnt anything about the craft's limits. They've learnt that distraction has consequences. A valid lesson, but not one that requires repeated demonstration.

The accidents worth having, if any accidents are worth having, are the ones that come from trying something at the edge of your current ability. From attempting a challenging cut. From pushing the wall thickness to see how thin you can go. From experimenting with form or proportion.

These accidents reveal your current limits and the information you need to expand them. The accidents that come from not paying attention or not following safety protocols just teach you to be more careful. A valuable lesson the first time, but not one that needs constant reinforcement.

The question isn't whether you'll have accidents. The question is what you'll do with them. Will you hide them, pretend they didn't happen, move on as quickly as possible? Or will you examine them, understand them, and extract the lessons they contain?

Will you let fear of accidents constrain your development, keeping you in safe territory where you never push boundaries? Or will you accept accidents as inevitable companions on the journey toward better work?

Accidents are uncomfortable teachers, certainly. But they're thorough, effective, and honest. They show you exactly where your limits are, precisely what you don't yet understand, and exactly what needs more attention.

Keep your accidents. If not physically, then at least in memory. Photograph them, perhaps. Study them. Understand them. Let them inform your future work. They're proof you're pushing your personal boundaries, exploring your limits, and growing as a turner.

The perfect turner who never had an accident doesn't exist. The good turner who learns from every accident? That's achievable. That's the goal. That's what transforms accidents from disasters into valuable teachers.

10: Saving What Seems Lost

THERE'S A MOMENT every woodturner knows intimately when something goes wrong. A catch, a split, a miscalculation that removes too much material, any number of different things. Your heart sinks. Your first instinct is to stop, to set the piece aside, to mentally file it under "learning experience" and move on to something new.

But wait. Look at it again. Really look. Sometimes a piece that seems ruined is simply one that needs to become something different from what you planned. The art of recovery isn't about fixing mistakes. It's about seeing possibilities where plans have fallen apart.

Recovery is pivoting, adapting, and seeing what the piece might want to become given its new circumstances.

The challenge is recognising when recovery is possible and when it's wishful thinking. Not every mistake can be transformed into a feature. Some pieces are genuinely beyond saving. Learning to tell the difference is crucial to both your time at the lathe and your confidence.

The line between recovery and wishful thinking isn't always clear. But there are some guidelines. Good recovery addresses the mistake directly, incorporates it into a coherent design (or cuts it away completely and goes with a new idea), and results in something that looks intentional even if the path to get there was accidental.

Bad recovery is when you're clearly trying to hide the mistake, when each fix creates new problems requiring more fixes, when the final result looks like exactly what it is: a series of compromises piled on top of each other.

I've seen bad recovery in action. A turner catches the side

of a bowl, creating a small chip. Rather than addressing it directly, they try to sand it away, which creates a flat spot. They try to turn away the flat spot. They try to even it out, which changes the proportions. By the end, they've spent an hour chasing a problem that started as a five-minute fix, and the bowl looks like it's been worried at rather than crafted. The original chip would have been less noticeable than the accumulated attempts to hide it.

Let me give you some practical examples of good recovery, situations I've navigated or watched others navigate successfully.

A catch on the exterior of a bowl, creating a visible gouge. You may not be able to remove it without making the piece significantly smaller. But you can hide it in plain sight by turning it into a "belt" that can be filled with something like coffee grounds or metal powders or an applied texture with a rotary tool, perhaps.

Here's how this works in practice. You take the gouge mark and deliberately extend it around the entire circumference of the bowl, creating a shallow channel or groove. This might be three or four millimetres wide and a couple of millimetres deep. Then you mix your filling material (coffee grounds work beautifully for a dark line, or you can use metal powders, crusite stone, or coloured epoxy) with CA glue or epoxy resin, and work it into the channel. Once cured, you sand it back flush with the surface. What was a random gouge becomes an intentional decorative band. The catch becomes the start of a design element. People will assume you planned it. The wood will know better, but wood keeps secrets.

A split or crack developing in the rim. You can cut the whole rim off, making the bowl shorter but intact. You can stabilise the crack with CA glue and incorporate it as a natural feature. You can create a cutout design that uses the split as a starting point. Multiple valid approaches are feasible a lot of the time, each one leading to different results, all better than declaring the piece unsalvageable.

The proportions go wrong. What was supposed to be a deep bowl is now shallow, or vice versa. Don't try to force it back to your original plan. Accept the new proportions (or change them completely) and refine them. A shallow bowl can be elegant if you commit to it. A deep bowl can be dramatic if you embrace it. The problem is usually the in-between state where you're neither fully here nor fully there.

These pivots require letting go of your original vision, which can be emotionally difficult. You had a plan. You were invested in that plan. Abandoning it feels like failure even when the alternative might be better than what you originally intended.

This is where ego becomes the enemy of recovery. If you're too attached to being right, to having your original plan succeed, you'll miss opportunities to salvage good work from imperfect circumstances. The piece doesn't care about your ego. The wood doesn't care if you stick to your plan. Only you care, and that caring can blind you to better alternatives.

I've found the best approach is to give yourself permission to grieve the lost plan, then move on to problem-solving. Yes, that catch ruins the clean line you wanted. Acknowledge the disappointment. Feel it. Then ask: given where we are now, what's possible?

This question, "given where we are now, what's possible?", is perhaps the most important question in recovery work. It accepts reality. It doesn't waste energy on what should have been. It focuses on what can be, given current circumstances.

Sometimes the answer is: *Nothing Good*. Sometimes the piece really is beyond recovery. Learning to recognise these situations, to not waste hours on hopeless causes, is part of developing judgement.

But more often than beginners expect, the answer is: quite a lot, actually. With creativity, with willingness to adapt, with openness to unexpected directions, many pieces that seem ruined can become good work. Different work than planned, certainly. But good nonetheless.

There's also a timing element to recovery. Some mistakes need immediate attention. That catch that's still fresh, a decision point where you need to commit to a direction. Other mistakes benefit from time. Step away, let your mind process the possibilities, then come back with fresh eyes.

I've saved pieces I initially thought were hopeless by simply putting them aside for a week or a month. When I return, the emotional attachment to the failed plan has faded. I can see the piece more objectively, see possibilities I couldn't see when I was still mourning what I'd intended to make.

This patience, giving yourself time to recover from the mistake before attempting to recover the piece, can be crucial, particularly with expensive timbers. Rushed recovery attempts, made while you're still upset or frustrated, rarely work as well as considered approaches made from a calmer state.

At The Woodturning School, I sometimes deliberately make mistakes during demonstrations. Nothing dangerous, but catches and slips and miscalculations. Then I show students how I would recover. Not to show off, but to normalise the reality that mistakes happen to everyone and that recovery is a standard skill, not an emergency measure.

I remember one demonstration where I was shaping the outside of a bowl and got distracted answering a question. The tool dipped and left a noticeable flat spot in what should have been a smooth curve. Rather than pretending it hadn't happened, I stopped and said, "Right, that wasn't intentional. Let's talk about options." We discussed whether to turn it away (would make the bowl noticeably smaller), incorporate it as a feature (didn't really suit this piece), or adjust the entire curve to accommodate it (the option I chose). The students got to see the thinking process in real time, the weighing of alternatives, the decision and commitment. That taught them more than a flawless demonstration would have.

These demonstrations do more for students' confidence than perfect demonstrations could. They see that mistakes aren't always catastrophic. They see that recovery is often possible. They see the thinking process: assess the situation, consider options, make a decision, and commit to it.

Recovery is a core skill, as important as good tool control or proper sanding technique. Because no matter how skilled you become, things will go wrong. The lathe will teach you humility.

The difference between a frustrated turner and a resilient one is that the latter has developed the skills, creativity, and emotional flexibility to recover from mistakes effectively.

So when something goes wrong, don't immediately despair. Stop. Look at what actually happened rather than what you wish had happened. Ask yourself what's possible given current circumstances. Consider multiple approaches. Choose one that makes sense, then commit to it.

Sometimes your recovery will transform a mistake into a feature, creating something more interesting than your original plan. Sometimes it will salvage acceptable work from what seemed like disaster. Sometimes it will teach you that this particular piece isn't recoverable, but the next one will be, because you'll have learnt from this attempt.

All of these outcomes are valuable. All of them make you a better turner. Recovery isn't just about saving pieces. It's about developing resilience, creativity, and the ability to adapt when circumstances change.

The art of recovery is another skill you develop through practice, through trying different approaches, through learning what works and what doesn't. It's creative problem-solving under pressure, with materials that won't cooperate and plans that have already failed.

But it's also deeply satisfying when it works. Taking a piece that seemed ruined and finding a way forward. There's a particular satisfaction in that, different from the satisfaction of perfect execution. It's the satisfaction of resourcefulness, of not giving up, of seeing possibilities others might miss.

So embrace recovery as a skill worth developing. Don't just learn to avoid mistakes, although that's important too. Learn to recover from them when they happen. Learn to see possibilities in problems. Learn to adapt when plans fall apart.

This resilience, this refusal to accept defeat at the first setback, these are qualities that will serve you well in woodturning. They'll serve you well in everything else too. The lathe teaches many lessons. Recovery is one of the most valuable.

11: What the Wood Knows

WOOD ISN'T A blank canvas. It's a collaborator with its own history, its own character, its own ideas about what it wants to become. The turners who consistently produce compelling work aren't the ones who impose their will on wood most forcefully. They're the ones who have learnt to read what the wood is telling them.

This reading, this conversation between maker and material, starts long before you mount anything on the lathe. It starts the moment you pick up a piece of wood, feel its weight, examine its surface, begin to understand what it might offer and what it might resist.

I had a revelation about this early in my turning journey, though I didn't recognise it as revelation at the time. I was working with a piece of ash, a decent-looking blank with no obvious flaws. Mounted it, brought it up to speed, took my first cut.

The wood grabbed my tool in a way that made no sense given what I was doing. It was the same cut I'd made successfully hundreds of times. Same tool, same angle, same approach. Different response.

I stopped, examined the surface, looked more carefully at the grain. And there it was. The grain wasn't running the direction the outside of the blank suggested. There was twist in the wood, invisible until I started cutting, that completely changed how the fibres wanted to be approached.

What I'd missed was subtle. The growth rings on the end grain showed a slight spiral, and when I looked at the side of the blank more carefully, I could see the grain lines weren't as I expected. They curved gently, which meant the fibres were twisting through the piece. My standard approach, which assumed straight grain, was fighting the wood's actual structure.

The wood had been telling me something. I just hadn't been paying attention.

Some wood is cooperative. It cuts cleanly, sands smoothly, finishes beautifully. This wood is teaching you what right feels like, how tools should behave when everything is working. Other wood is difficult. It tears, it catches, it fights every cut. This wood is also teaching, though the lessons are different. It's showing you the limits of your technique, revealing where your skills need development. The point isn't to avoid difficult wood but to learn from both types. Easy wood builds confidence. Difficult wood builds capability. Both are necessary for growth.

Let's start with grain direction, because it's both the most important and the most misunderstood aspect of reading wood.

Reading this grain means looking at the blank before you start, tracking how the growth rings run, watching for transitions where the direction may change. It means maybe adjusting your approach when you feel the wood resisting, recognising that resistance as information rather than obstacle.

This means understanding that different areas of your bowl will cut differently. The end grain sections will be harder, the long grain sections will be softer, more forgiving. Moving from one to the other as your tool travels around the form, you're constantly aware of the difference in cut. Often unconsciously once you've developed the feel for it.

But before unconscious adjustment can happen, conscious awareness must develop. You need to deliberately observe how the wood responds in different areas. Feel when your tool is cutting easily versus when it's working harder. Watch the shavings. They change character as you move through different grain orientations. Long, curling ribbons from the long grain sections. Shorter, more crumbly chips from the end grain. The shavings are telling you what's happening at the cutting edge.

Take spalted wood. The dark zone lines that create those stunning patterns are created by fungi, which softens the wood in unpredictable ways. You'll be cutting through solid wood, then suddenly hit a soft spot, then back to solid. Your tool wants to dig into the soft sections, requiring constant vigilance and adjustment.

Burrs present different challenges. The grain swirls in every direction simultaneously. There's no "with the grain" cutting. You're always partially against it no matter which way you approach. The solution is sharp tools, light cuts, and acceptance that some tear-out is inevitable. You're managing it, not eliminating it.

Different species have different voices too. Cherry is quiet and cooperative. Oak is loud and demanding. Olivewood is dense and resistant. Each species has characteristic behaviours. Learning these characteristics takes time, but it makes working with each species more effective because you know what to expect and how to respond.

There's also the matter of moisture content. Wet wood and dry wood behave completely differently. Wet wood cuts more easily but moves dramatically as it dries. Dry wood is harder to cut but stable. Understanding moisture content and how it affects your work is crucial.

You can't necessarily read moisture content visually, though fresh-cut wood often has obvious signs like end checking or visible moisture on the surface. But you can feel it as you cut. Wet wood produces continuous shavings, has a distinctive smell (fresh and almost sweet with many species), feels almost soft under your tools. Wet wood is also easy to tell as it has a tendency to give you and your lathe a shower. Over-dry wood produces dust more than shavings, feels harder, creates more heat from friction.

I once tried to finish turn a bowl that wasn't fully dry. It looked dry, felt dry, seemed ready. But as I worked, the wood began fuzzing badly, with surface fibres pulling up rather than cutting clean. The wood was telling me it was still too wet. I should have listened immediately. Instead, I fought it, trying to force clean cuts. The result was hours of extra sanding to fix surface quality that would have been fine if I'd just waited for proper drying.

This reading informs your decisions. If the wood is wet and you want a stable final piece, you have options. Rough-turn it to about 10% of the diameter in wall thickness and set it aside to dry for weeks or months before final turning. Or turn it thin and accept the distortion that will occur (and possibly splitting), making it a feature rather than a flaw. Or stabilise it with a penetrating finish immediately to slow the drying and minimise movement. The wood's current state, combined with what you want to achieve, determines which approach makes sense.

Temperature affects wood too. Cold wood is harder, more brittle. Warm wood is slightly softer, more forgiving. This is subtle, but noticeable if you're paying attention. Winter workshop versus summer workshop produces different cutting experiences with the same wood species. The wood is responding to temperature, and that response affects how you should work it.

Defects also need reading. Checks, splits, bark inclusions, worm holes. They're not necessarily problems. They can be features, if you work with them rather than trying to eliminate them. But you need to understand what they are and how they'll affect your turning.

A check in a bowl blank might need stabilising with CA glue before turning. Or it might become a design element. Or it might indicate where the wood will split further, meaning you should plan your design to either incorporate that split or avoid the area entirely.

Reading defects means understanding their nature. A stress check, which is a radial split from the pith, will likely grow as you turn. A shake, which is a separation between growth rings, might be stable or might open up under turning forces. Bark inclusions might be loose or tight. Each tells you something about how to proceed.

Wood also tells you when it's time to stop. A piece that has been turned to appropriate thickness will have a particular resonance when tapped. Too thick and it sounds dead. Too thin and it sounds nervous. Listening to this acoustic feedback helps judge wall thickness without calipers.

Here's what to listen for. Tap the wall of your bowl with a knuckle or the handle of a tool. A thick wall produces a dull thud, the sound absorbed by the mass of material. As walls thin, the pitch rises and the sound becomes more resonant, almost musical. There's a sweet spot where the bowl rings with a clear, sustained note. That's usually good thickness for most functional work. If you go thinner still, the sound becomes higher and shorter, almost tinny, and you can hear a nervousness in it, a sense of fragility. That's your warning that you're approaching the limits.

I learnt this from pottery. Potters tap their pots to judge wall thickness by sound. The same principle applies to turned wood. The sound tells you about the material's state. Developing an ear for this acoustic information adds another sense to your toolkit, not relying solely on vision or touch but also incorporating hearing.

The sound of cutting itself is also communication. A smooth, consistent sound indicates clean cutting. A stuttering or grinding sound suggests problems: dull tool, inappropriate angle, or difficult grain. Learning to hear these differences allows you to respond to problems the moment they begin rather than waiting until visual evidence appears.

I can often diagnose student problems by sound before looking at their work. A sharp tool cutting well produces a clean, almost singing tone, consistent and smooth[24]. A dull tool sounds duller, with more friction in the sound, almost a scraping rather than slicing quality. A tool that's about to catch makes a rising, tightening sound as it begins to dig in. If you hear that change and pull back immediately, you can often prevent the catch from completing. A tool rubbing the bevel without cutting sounds like a hollow banging, without the substance of a proper cut. These distinctions become obvious once you start listening for them.

This might sound mystical or overly romantic, treating wood as communication. But it's entirely practical. Material properties determine tool behaviour. Those properties express themselves through feedback. Paying attention to that feedback and responding appropriately is simply good technique, regardless of whether you frame it as listening to wood or as material science.

I prefer the listening framing because it encourages attention and respect. Thinking of wood as a material to be dominated leads to forcing and fighting. Thinking of wood as something to listen to encourages adaptation and collaboration. Both framings describe the same physical reality, but one produces a better relationship with the work.

This reading ability develops over time, over hundreds of pieces turned, over countless observations made and remembered. You can't force it. You can't learn it from a book, though you can learn what to look for. The actual reading, the intuitive understanding of what wood is telling you, comes only with experience.

So learn to read wood. Not just as a technical exercise, but as relationship building. Wood is your collaborator in this work. It brings as much to the partnership as you do. The turners who produce the most compelling work aren't necessarily the most technically skilled. They're the ones who have learnt to read what the wood is offering and respond appropriately.

Pay attention. Look carefully. Feel deliberately. Listen closely. Let each piece teach you its lessons. Over time, this attention becomes instinct. You'll pick up a blank and immediately understand its character, its potential, its challenges. Not consciously analysing, just knowing.

That's the goal. Not perfect reading, because wood will always surprise you. But informed reading, where you understand what you're working with well enough to make good decisions, to avoid unnecessary battles, to create pieces that honour the material.

The wood speaks. Learn its language. Listen to what it tells you. Your work will be better for it[25].

12: Edges and Boundaries

A PIECE OF wood becomes a turning when you remove material. But it becomes compelling when people want to touch and hold and live with it, often through how they handle its edges. The rim of a bowl, the transition where a curve meets a foot, the line where wood meets space. These boundaries define the piece as much as its overall form does.

I learnt this lesson through failure, which seems to be how I learn most of my important lessons. Early in my turning career, I'd focus obsessively on the main form. Getting the bowl's curve right, achieving good proportions, managing wall thickness. The rim was an afterthought, the detail I'd get to last if I had time.

My pieces looked fine. Correct. Competent. Also completely forgettable.

Then I saw a demonstration by a turner whose work I admired. I watched him spend time on a bowl's rim. Refining it, checking it with his fingers, making tiny adjustments. The actual bowl was complete in a short enough time. He then spent a few minutes just on the rim detail.

I started paying attention after that. Started noticing how different rim treatments affected my response to pieces. A sharp edge made a bowl feel aggressive, modern, crisp. A rounded edge felt softer, more traditional, inviting. A slightly undercut rim created a shadow line, adding visual interest.

These weren't huge differences. We're talking millimetres of detail. But their impact on the piece's overall character was enormous. The same bowl form with different rim treatments felt like different pieces entirely[26].

So let's talk about edges systematically, because they're more complex than they first appear.

The rim of a bowl is the obvious starting point. You have choices here, each creating different effects. A simple square edge is exactly what it sounds like: the exterior surface meets the interior surface at a crisp right angle. This is clean, modern, and shows your turning skill since there's nowhere to hide imperfections.

But square edges are also harsh. They catch light sharply, feel abrupt to the touch. They work beautifully for contemporary forms where you want that crisp precision. They're less suitable for organic, natural-edge pieces where softness is the goal.

A rounded edge softens everything. The exterior curves to meet the interior in a smooth transition. This is traditional, comfortable, easy on the eye and hand. It's also more forgiving to create. Small irregularities disappear into the curve rather than standing out as they would on a square edge.

The challenge with rounded edges is making them consistent. It's easy to create a round-ish edge that varies in radius around the rim. What looks fine in one spot reads as sloppy when the whole rim is inconsistent. This is where touch becomes crucial. Running your fingers around the rim reveals variations your eyes might miss.

Then there are compound edges, combinations of different treatments. A slight flat section before the curve. A bead detail. A gentle undercut. These add visual interest, create shadow lines, give character to what might otherwise be simple.

Beyond rims, there are other edges to consider. The foot of a bowl, where it meets the table or shelf. This is another boundary that deserves attention. A sharp edge can look crisp but also feels precarious, like the piece might scratch surfaces. A chamfered or rounded edge may feel more finished, more considered.

The size of the foot matters too. Too small and the piece looks unstable, makes people nervous. Too large and it dominates, draws attention away from the form. Finding that balance, where the foot provides adequate support without calling attention to itself, is part of developing an eye for proportion.

As a rough guide, I often start with a foot diameter around one-third of the rim diameter, then adjust based on the piece's visual weight. A heavy, solid form might need a larger foot to look grounded. A delicate, thin-walled piece can get away with something smaller. The foot should feel inevitable when you look at it, neither too much nor too little, just right for that particular form.

The treatment of the foot's edge follows similar principles to the rim. A small chamfer, just a millimetre or two at 45 degrees, prevents the sharp edge that catches on surfaces and chips easily. A gentle radius creates a softer appearance. The choice depends on the character you're creating. A contemporary piece might want crisp, defined edges throughout. A traditional piece might want everything softened and rounded.

Then there are transition points, where one curve meets another, where a straight section becomes a curve, where form changes direction. These boundaries aren't edges in the tactile sense, but they function as visual edges, defining where one element ends and another begins.

Sharp transitions create energy, visual interest, clear definition. Soft transitions feel organic, flowing, peaceful. Neither is inherently better. The question is: what does this particular piece want? What character are you trying to create?

This decision-making, understanding how different edge treatments affect a piece's character, develops through observation. Look at work you admire. Really look at it. Not just the overall form but the details. How are the edges handled? What effect does that treatment create? Could you achieve similar effects in your work?

I keep a mental catalogue of edge treatments I've seen and admired. These observations inform my choices. When I'm working on a piece, I have options in my mental database to draw from. This choice isn't random. It's informed by what I've observed works in similar contexts.

There's also the practical matter of how to create clean edges consistently. This is technique, and technique matters enormously. A beautiful edge treatment executed poorly looks worse than a simple treatment executed well.

For bowl rims, I typically work from the interior side, cutting a clean chamfer or radius before final sanding. This gives me clear access and good control. The tool approach matters here. For a rounded edge, I use a small gouge or spindle gouge, presenting it at an angle that lets me roll the edge rather than cut it flat. The motion is almost a scooping action, curving from the interior wall up and over the rim in one smooth pass. Multiple light passes build the radius gradually rather than trying to create it in one aggressive cut.

For a sharp, square edge, the approach is different. I'll refine each surface separately, the interior wall and the exterior, bringing them as close to the rim as I can with clean, controlled cuts. The final edge is then refined with abrasives rather than tools, carefully maintaining that crisp meeting point without rounding it over accidentally.

The final edge is then refined with progressive grits, working methodically until it's silky smooth. The sanding on edges is crucial. It's easy to rush this. The piece is nearly done, you're eager to finish, the edge is just a detail. But inadequate sanding shows immediately. Run your fingers around a rim and you'll feel every scratch, every rough spot, every place you hurried.

I sand edges separately from main surfaces, giving them dedicated attention. For rims, I'll often fold the abrasive and work it along the edge specifically, feeling for consistency as I go. The pressure needs to be even all the way around, which is harder than it sounds when you're reaching across a spinning bowl. Some turners stop the lathe and sand edges by hand for better control. Either approach works if you're thorough.

This isn't inefficient. It's acknowledging that edges are tactile experiences as much as visual ones. People will touch your work's edges first. Make sure that experience is good.

Boundaries also exist in design decisions: where you choose to add detail versus leave plain, where pattern ends, where colour transitions occur if you're adding surface decoration. These aren't physical edges you can touch, but they function as compositional boundaries that organise the piece visually.

Handling these boundaries well means understanding visual weight and balance. A band of texture around a bowl's exterior creates a boundary between textured and smooth. Where you place that boundary affects the piece's proportions, its visual stability, its character. Too high and it looks top-heavy. Too low and it might look indecisive.

These decisions about where boundaries occur, how they're treated, and what character they create are what separate adequate work from compelling work. Technical skill gets you to adequate. Design sensitivity, attention to detail, understanding of how boundaries affect character: these get you to compelling.

So pay attention to your edges. The rim that meets hand and lip. The foot that meets the surface. The transitions where one form element meets another. The boundaries where decorated meets plain, where detail lives and where it's absent.

These aren't afterthoughts. They're not the details you get to if you have time. They're fundamental to your piece's character, to how it will be experienced, to whether it's merely correct or actually compelling.

Make them clean. Make them intentional. Make them consistent. Give them the time and attention they deserve. Your work will show the difference. Not in obvious ways necessarily, but in the subtle ways that separate good work from excellent work.

Edges and boundaries define your piece as much as its overall form[27]. Learn to handle them well, and you'll create work that people want to touch, to hold, to keep. Work that feels finished and considered rather than just technically complete.

The details matter. The edges matter. The boundaries matter. Pay attention to them, and your work will show that attention in ways that speak quietly but powerfully.

Working on a piece for a project, paying close attention to the shape I'm creating. 2025.

Part Three

What the Heart Feels

Technique and thought only take you so far. At some point, the work becomes about something deeper: the feel of a cut that's right, the rhythm that emerges through repetition, the instinct for when shape serves purpose, the pulse of sustainable practice, the composure needed when things go wrong, and the care that shows in how something ends. This chapter explores the emotional and intuitive dimensions of making, the knowledge that lives below conscious thought.

13: Loving the Work

THERE'S A QUESTION people sometimes ask when they visit the workshop: why do you do this? They're looking at the shavings on the floor, the dust in the air, the hours invested in something that could be bought for less than the cost of the wood. It's a fair question. The economics don't make sense. The time doesn't make sense. And yet here I am, over a decade in, still showing up at the lathe, teaching, demonstrating and running my woodturning business.

The honest answer is that I love it. Not in some abstract, philosophical way, but in the immediate, physical sense of enjoying the doing. The weight of a tool in my hands. The smell of fresh-cut oak. The moment when a curve finally resolves into something that feels right. These small pleasures accumulate into something larger, a life that feels meaningful in ways that are hard to articulate but easy to feel.

I didn't expect this when I started. I expected to learn a skill, maybe produce some nice objects, but still with the goal of becoming a professional. The lathe became a place where time worked differently, where the noise in my head would quiet, where I could be fully present in a way that the rest of life rarely permitted.

There's a state of absorption that happens at the lathe, one you'll have experienced if you've been turning for any length of time. Time disappears. The mental noise quiets. We'll explore this more fully later in the book, but for now, know that this is one of the great gifts of the craft.

But I think there's something more specific to working

with hands and material that amplifies the joy. Research into craft and wellbeing consistently finds that making things provides psychological benefits beyond what we'd expect from the activity alone[28].

Creating something tangible, something you can hold and use, seems to satisfy a need that more abstract work doesn't reach. There's pride in the making. There's the pleasure of competence developed over time. And there's something that settles in you when you've spent hours shaping wood into form.

The joy also comes from the relationship with material. Wood was alive. It grew for decades or centuries, responding to seasons, to weather, to the particular conditions of its place. Now it's in my hands, and I get to collaborate with that history. Every piece is different. Every piece teaches something. The grain runs unexpectedly, the figure reveals itself as I cut, the colour deepens as oil soaks in. There's constant discovery, constant conversation.

I've watched this same joy appear in students. There's a moment, usually partway through the lesson, when something shifts. They stop thinking about technique and start feeling the work. Their shoulders drop. Their breathing slows. They're present in a way they might not have been for weeks. It's visible from across the workshop.

One student told me afterwards that she hadn't felt that calm in months. She'd come to learn a skill and discovered something else entirely: a place where her anxious mind could rest. She wasn't unusual. Research suggests that craft activities can have genuine therapeutic effects, reducing stress and anxiety while increasing feelings of wellbeing.[29] The repetitive, focused nature of the work seems to engage something similar to meditation.

This doesn't mean every moment at the lathe is blissful. There's frustration when things go wrong. There's tedium in some operations. There's the physical tiredness after a long session. Joy isn't the absence of difficulty. It's the presence of meaning that makes the difficulty worthwhile.

I think about why I keep doing this, year after year, and the answer keeps coming back to something simple: it makes me happy. Not in a giddy, excitable way, but in a deeper sense of life being well spent. The hours at the lathe feel like good hours. The work feels like good work. Whatever I produce, whatever I sell or give away or keep, the real value is in the doing.

The philosopher Richard Sennett writes that the craftsman represents a basic human impulse: the desire to do a job well for its own sake.[30] That rings true. When I'm turning well, I'm not thinking about outcomes or audiences or what the piece might be worth. I'm absorbed in the work itself. The satisfaction is intrinsic. The motivation comes from within.

This intrinsic motivation matters more than I initially understood. External rewards, like money or recognition, can actually undermine the joy of work if they become the primary focus.[31] The research on this is clear: people who engage in activities primarily for external rewards often find less enjoyment than those who engage for the activity's own sake. Turning for the love of turning produces better experiences than turning for the gallery or the commission. This doesn't mean I don't appreciate when work sells or when someone values what I've made. But that's not why I do it. I do it because the doing itself is worthwhile.

There's also joy in the community. Woodturning could be solitary, and sometimes I treasure the solitude. But the connections with other turners, whether through teaching, through clubs, through the strange camaraderie of people who understand why you'd spend a Saturday covered in wood chips, add another dimension of pleasure. Shared enthusiasm amplifies individual joy. Watching someone else's breakthrough feels nearly as good as your own.

The love of work isn't something that arrives fully formed. It develops through practice, through showing up regularly, through the gradual accumulation of skill and understanding. Early sessions were more struggle than joy. I was too busy trying not to make mistakes to feel much pleasure. But as competence grew, space opened up for enjoyment. The work stopped being effortful and started being absorbing. This progression seems common. The joy is earned through persistence.

I've also learnt that joy needs protecting. It's possible to turn the love of something into obligation, to overcommit until the pleasure drains away. I do my best to guard against this. I pay attention to when turning feels like a gift and when it starts feeling like a burden. I adjust accordingly where possible. The workshop should remain a place I want to be, not a place I have to be. That distinction matters.

When conditions align, when I'm rested and focused, when the wood cooperates and the tools are sharp, there are sessions where hours pass like minutes. I emerge slightly dazed, blinking at the clock, wondering where the afternoon went. And I feel more alive than I did when I started. That's the gift. That's why I do this. That's the joy at the lathe.

14: Again and Again

THERE'S MAGIC IN making the same thing multiple times. Not because repetition leads to perfection, but because it reveals nuance. The first time you make something, you're figuring it out. The fifth time, you're refining. The fiftieth time, you're discovering.

I remember when I first decided to make a series of bowls from the same blank size, aiming for the same form. I thought by the tenth one I'd be bored. Instead, I was fascinated. Each bowl taught me something new about the relationship between tool angle and surface quality, about how slight changes in curve affected visual weight, and about how my body could learn efficiency through repetition.

Repetition isn't about making identical objects. It's about deepening your understanding[32]. Every iteration teaches you something the previous one couldn't because you're approaching it with slightly more knowledge, slightly more muscle memory, slightly more confidence.

When I teach, I often suggest students make the same piece on their own lathe three or four times in a session. The resistance is immediate. Why make the same thing again when I could make something new? But by the third attempt, they'll understand. The first piece was struggle. The second was competence. The third revealed possibilities they hadn't seen before because they were no longer consumed by basic execution.

This is true across all making disciplines. Potters throw the same form hundreds of times. Blacksmiths forge the same joint repeatedly. Musicians practice the same passage until it becomes fluid. The repetition isn't mindless. It's how skill embeds itself in the body, how understanding moves from conscious thought to intuitive action.

Students often want variety. They want to make a bowl, then a box, then a vessel, then something else. This is natural. Novelty is exciting, and making different things exposes you to different challenges. But there's deep learning available in repetition that novelty can't provide. Novelty teaches breadth; repetition teaches depth.

When you make the same thing repeatedly, you remove variables. You're not learning how to hollow a box and how to shape a bowl at the same time. You're learning how to hollow this box, with this wood, at this moment, building on what you learnt the last time you hollowed this box. The learning compounds rather than resets.

I see this dramatically in production turners. Someone making a living turning pepper mills or honey dippers or bowls for a wholesale account will make the same item hundreds or thousands of times. To an outsider, this looks tedious. To the maker, each piece is an opportunity to refine, to experiment with tiny variations, to find ways to work more efficiently or more beautifully.

The best production turners I know aren't bored. They're deeply engaged. They've moved past the basic questions of how and into the subtle questions of why this way versus that way, what happens if I adjust this slightly, how can I make this easier on my body, what does this particular piece of wood want to become within these constraints.

These tiny variations matter more than you'd think. A production turner might experiment with starting the curve half a millimetre higher, or using a slightly different tool angle on the final pass, or changing the sequence of cuts to reduce sanding. To an outsider, the bowls look identical. To the maker, each one is a small experiment. Does this adjustment make the form more pleasing? Does it save thirty seconds per piece? Does it reduce strain on the wrist? Over hundreds of pieces, these refinements accumulate into significant improvements in both quality and efficiency.

There's also a meditative quality to skilled repetition. When you know the form intimately, when your hands remember the movements, you enter a flow state where thinking and doing merge[33]. This isn't possible with constant novelty because novelty demands conscious attention. Repetition, paradoxically, frees attention for subtler observations.

I notice this when demonstrating. I can turn a familiar form while talking, answering questions, observing the audience, and having a great time whilst doing it. My hands know what to do. This automaticity only develops through repetition, through making the same cuts enough times that they become encoded in muscle memory rather than requiring conscious direction.

This doesn't mean the work becomes mechanical. Even with deep familiarity, each piece of wood is unique. The grain runs differently. The density varies. Small checks or knots appear unexpectedly. So while the form is repetitive, the execution is always responsive. You're repeating the intention, not the exact actions.

There's also the question of what to repeat. Some makers repeat forms. Others repeat techniques, practising the same cut on different projects until it becomes reliable. Still others repeat processes, developing a systematic approach to surface preparation or finishing that they apply consistently. All of these have value.

I tend to repeat forms when I'm trying to understand something specific about proportion or curve. I'll make variations on a theme: bowls with slightly different rim diameters, or slightly different wall thicknesses, or slightly different base proportions. This focused repetition teaches me how small changes affect the overall impression.

I'm certainly not a production turner, the idea of turning 'x' number of the same pieces for one job fills me with dread and it's not what I became a turner for. I have huge respect for those who do, like Les Thorne who shares the workshop with me. To watch him work with the same precision time and again, sometimes turning hundreds of the same thing and not complaining as much as you might think, is something to behold.

When I was developing the projects for Woodturning Form and Formula, I made several of versions of each piece. Not because I needed that many, but because each iteration revealed something about why certain proportions worked better than others. The repetition was research, a way of testing ideas through making rather than just through thinking. Each served as a practice piece so I could demonstrate the process fluently for an audience.

There's humility in repetition too. It reminds you that mastery isn't a destination but a process. No matter how many times you make something, there's always room for refinement. The hundredth bowl can still teach you something if you're paying attention.

I remember talking to Les who'd been making the same thing for a few days. Hundreds of the same piece. I asked if he was bored yet. He looked surprised. Bored? No. "I just love making wood round", he said as if I should have known the answer.

This perspective shift matters. If you view repetition as doing the same thing over and over, it becomes tedious. If you view it as returning to the same challenge with accumulated understanding, it becomes fascinating. The form stays the same; your relationship with it evolves.

Repetition also builds confidence. The first time you attempt something, uncertainty dominates. Will this work? Can I do this? By the tenth attempt, those questions fade. You know you can do it. The question becomes how well, and that's a more interesting question to explore.

There's also practical value in repetition. If you want to make something for sale, or as a gift, or for yourself to use daily, you need to be able to make it reliably. Repetition develops that reliability. It turns a lucky success into a repeatable skill. A repeated skill means more efficiency and you can turn the piece quicker and sell it for an affordable price whilst still maintaining a good profit margin. This is a discussion for a different platform than this book, but it is worth thinking seriously about. Too many turners sell their work for not much more than the price of the blank, which, in my opinion, undermines the skill required and the craft in general… There, I said it!

I encourage students to choose one form and make it ten times before moving on. Not necessarily all at once, but over a period of weeks or months. By the tenth version, they'll understand that form in a way the first version couldn't provide. They'll have opinions about it. Preferences about proportions, feelings about how it should curve, ideas about variations worth exploring.

This depth of engagement is what separates someone who has made something from someone who knows how to make something. The difference is repetition, returning to the same challenge enough times that it becomes familiar territory rather than uncertain ground.

Repetition also teaches you about your own patterns. You discover that you tend to make walls too thick, or bases too narrow, or rims too sharp. These tendencies only become visible through repetition. Once you see them, you can choose whether to correct them or embrace them as part of your style.

Here's how to spot your patterns. Line up your repeated pieces and really look at them. Measure them if you need to. Where are they consistent? Where do they vary? The consistencies are your ingrained habits, some intentional, some not. I discovered through this process that I consistently make feet slightly too large. Every bowl, the foot was about five millimetres bigger than the proportion guidelines suggested. Once I saw it, I had to decide: was this a flaw to correct or a preference to own? I decided it was a preference. I like a solid, grounded look. But I couldn't have made that decision without the repetition revealing the pattern.

There's also the question of when to stop repeating. At some point, you've extracted what you can from a particular form or technique. Continuing becomes habit rather than exploration. This is when novelty serves. It refreshes your attention, presents new challenges, prevents stagnation. The art is knowing when repetition serves learning and when it becomes avoidance of new challenges.

The value of repetition extends beyond specific forms or techniques. It applies to process too. Developing consistent approaches to mounting work, to sharpening tools, to finishing surfaces. These repeated processes build efficiency and reliability. You're not thinking about how to do them; you're doing them while thinking about other things.

This is how professionals work. They've systematised the repetitive elements so they can focus attention on the variables: this particular piece of wood, this particular design challenge, this particular client request. The foundation is automatic; the creativity happens on top of that foundation.

Every repetition is an opportunity to go deeper, to refine understanding, to build skill that compounds rather than resets. The form may be the same, but you're not. That's the value of repetition. It reveals how much you've changed by keeping everything else constant.

15: Why Shape Matters

A BOWL THAT can't hold what it's meant to hold has failed, no matter how beautiful its curves. A handle that's uncomfortable to grip compromises the entire piece. Form and function aren't opposing forces. They're partners in good design.

I learnt this lesson through use, not theory. I made platters that were too flat to hold food without spilling. I made boxes whose lids stuck or fell off. I made vessels so delicate they couldn't be handled without anxiety. Each failure taught me that aesthetic appeal without practical function is incomplete.

The boxes taught me about tolerance and wood movement. I'd made lids that fitted perfectly when I finished them, with that satisfying pop of a snug fit. A month later, after the wood had moved with changing humidity, some were stuck so tight they needed prying open. Others had shrunk until they rattled loose. I learnt that a perfect fit at the lathe isn't always a perfect fit in real life. Function means thinking about how the piece will behave over time, not just how it looks when it leaves the workshop.

This doesn't mean every piece must be utilitarian. Sculptural work has its own validity. But even sculptural pieces have function. They must stand, must balance, must invite interaction or contemplation. The function might be emotional rather than practical, but it must exist.

When I start a piece, I ask myself what it needs to do. If it's a bowl, it needs to hold things without tipping. If it's a vessel, it needs to feel balanced in the hand. If it's decorative, it needs to reward close observation. These functional requirements inform every design decision that follows.

There's something interesting that happens when you make enough pieces. Some of them look right, and some of them don't. You can't always explain why in the moment. The form just feels resolved, or it doesn't.

For years, I thought this was instinct. Perhaps some innate sense of proportion that either you had or you didn't. But the more I paid attention, and the more I studied pieces that worked (my own and others'), the clearer the pattern became. Behind almost every piece that looked right lay a familiar set of proportions: the Golden Ratio[34] and the Rule of Thirds[35].

The Rule of Thirds is the simpler of the two. Imagine dividing your piece into three equal horizontal sections. Where the key transitions happen, where the widest point sits, where the foot meets the body, often falls naturally at these third lines. It's straightforward, dependable, and if you've been turning for any length of time, you're probably already using it without realising.

The Golden Ratio is more subtle. It's that mysterious 1.618 proportion that appears everywhere in nature, from the spiral of a nautilus shell to the arrangement of seeds in a sunflower. In turning, it often shows up around the 62% mark, roughly five-eighths of the way up a form. When the widest point of a vessel sits there, when a transition happens at that height, the piece tends to feel naturally graceful rather than studied.

Here's what I find genuinely fascinating: when a piece looks right to your eye, there's a very good chance it already conforms to one of these proportions. You didn't necessarily plan it. You just kept adjusting the curve, refining the transition, until something clicked[36]. And when you measure it afterwards, there it is. The golden ratio. The rule of thirds. Hiding in plain sight.

This isn't mystical. It's accumulated experience

synthesised into instinct. Your brain processes proportions and curves faster than conscious thought, then presents you with a feeling of rightness or wrongness. Those classical proportions aren't arbitrary inventions. They're attempts to codify what humans have always found beautiful.

There's a satisfying discipline in letting these proportions guide your decisions. They narrow possibilities in useful ways. You're not working with infinite options; you're working within constraints that help you focus. The bowl needs a foot wide enough for stability. The box needs walls thick enough for strength. The vessel wants its widest point somewhere that feels balanced to the eye.

These requirements aren't limitations. They're foundations.

I've noticed that pieces designed with clear proportion in mind often end up more beautiful than pieces designed purely for appearance. There's an honesty to proportional design that reads as integrity. The form makes sense because it serves both purpose and pattern. It feels inevitable rather than arbitrary.

This is especially true with traditional forms. A mortar and pestle shaped for efficient grinding is beautiful because the form follows from both the function and natural proportion so directly. A handled vessel with proper balance and pourability has elegance that comes from solving its practical problems while respecting timeless ratios. Form following function and proportion produces a kind of beauty that decoration alone can't achieve.

Think about a simple bowl for a moment. If the foot's too small, the whole thing looks like it might topple over. Too large, and it drags the eye away from the rest of the form. The rim? Same story. Too thick and the piece feels clunky. Too thin and it looks fragile, even if it isn't structurally. But when you get the proportions right, when the curve flows and the form holds together, suddenly the bowl looks thoughtful, intentional, and elegant.

What 'right' usually means, when you analyse it, is that the major divisions fall somewhere close to those classical proportions. The foot might be roughly a third of the diameter. The height might relate to the width by something approaching the golden ratio. You didn't plan this with calipers and calculations. You just kept adjusting until it looked correct. The proportions were guiding you all along.

That said, function and proportion alone aren't sufficient. There are infinitely many ways to make a functional, well-proportioned bowl. The challenge is making one that's also beautiful, where the curves are pleasurable to look at, where the proportions feel balanced, where the surface invites touch. This is where craft becomes art.

I think of function as the foundation, proportion as the framework, and form as the refinement. Get the function right first. Make sure the piece can do what it needs to do. Let proportion guide your major decisions, your heights and widths and transitions. Then refine the form within those parameters. This sequence prevents the common mistake of creating something beautiful but impractical, and it gives you guardrails that actually help rather than hinder.

There are also cultural dimensions to form and function. What one culture considers functional, another might not. A tea bowl designed for Japanese tea ceremony has different functional requirements than a mug designed for morning coffee. Both are vessels for drinking, but their purposes shape their forms differently. Yet both traditions, when executed well, tend to arrive at forms that honour those same underlying proportions. The specific shapes differ, but the sense of rightness comes from the same place.

Understanding these contextual requirements is part of good design. If you're making something for a specific use or user, understanding how they will interact with it informs every decision. The form should enable the function, not fight it. And the proportions should support both.

There's also the question of how much function is enough. A bowl needs to hold contents and sit stably. Does it need to nest for storage? Does it need to stack? Each additional functional requirement shapes the design. Deciding which functions matter and which can be sacrificed is part of the design process.

I generally favour simplicity. If a piece can serve its primary function well without additional features, I leave them out. Extra features often compromise the purity of form. A lid that fits perfectly is more elegant than one bristling with too much additional detail. The function is served; the form is clean; the proportions aren't complicated by unnecessary additions.

That said, some pieces benefit from complexity. A box with a fitted lid and a small pull has more function than one without. The question is always whether the additional complexity serves the piece or just adds visual noise. Function justifies complexity; decoration doesn't always.

There's also durability to consider. A functional piece that breaks after one use has failed its function. This is where craft quality matters. Proper wall thickness, appropriate wood selection, suitable finishes. These technical decisions affect whether the piece can fulfil its function over time.

The wall thickness question comes up often with students. They see photos of impossibly thin-walled bowls and want to achieve the same thing. But those pieces are often display items, not functional ware. A salad bowl that will be used daily, washed, dried, and filled with heavy contents needs walls of at least six to eight millimetres depending on the species. Harder woods like oak or ash can go a bit thinner. Softer woods like sycamore need a bit more.

A decorative piece that sits on a shelf can be much thinner because it won't see the same stress. The function determines the appropriate thickness, not some abstract ideal of impressive thinness.

This doesn't mean everything should be robust to the point of clumsiness. There's grace in delicacy if it's appropriate to the function. A small decorative vessel can be delicate because it won't be handled roughly. A salad bowl needs to be sturdy because it will see heavy use. Matching fragility to purpose is part of thoughtful design.

Some turners resist thinking about proportion explicitly. They want to work by feel, by instinct, by eye. I understand the impulse. The mathematics can feel cold, and nobody wants their work to seem calculated rather than felt.

But here's what I've learnt: the principles are already there in work that succeeds. The Golden Ratio and the Rule of Thirds aren't restrictions we impose on good design. They're patterns we observe in good design. When you train your eye over years at the lathe, what you're really doing is internalising these proportions until they become instinct.

This confidence develops gradually. The proportions you once checked with calipers become something you feel rather than measure. When you stop treating principles as tests to pass and start experiencing them as foundations to build upon. When you realise that understanding the golden ratio means you can explore with it, play with it, let it inform your choices rather than dictate them.

I've watched this development in my own work. There was a time when I measured obsessively, checking every major dimension against the ratio. Now I rarely reach for calipers during the design phase. I look at what's emerging and I know whether it's working or needs adjustment. The measurements haven't disappeared from my process. They've just moved inside, become part of how I see rather than something I check against a formula.

When your technical knowledge empowers your intuition rather than limiting it, that's when things get interesting.

When you understand these proportions well enough that you can feel when a form is harmonious without measuring it. When you grasp balance and weight distribution so thoroughly that your eye automatically recognises when something is working.

I try to make pieces where form and function and proportion feel inseparable, where you can't imagine one without the others. The curve of a bowl rim is beautiful and functional for pouring and sits at a height that just looks right. The proportion of a box is pleasing and practical for what it stores and relates to the lid in a way that satisfies something deep in how we see.

When form, function, and proportion merge completely, the design feels inevitable.

Not form serving function, or proportion dictating form, but all three working together in service of the piece. That integration is what I aim for, and when it succeeds, the work feels complete in a way that any single element alone never achieves.

The beauty of understanding these proportions is that they don't restrict your creativity. They explain why your best instincts were right all along. They give you confidence that when something looks good to your eye, there's a reason it looks good. And they provide a framework for the days when instinct alone isn't quite getting you there.

Keep experimenting. Keep adjusting until it looks right. And trust that when it does look right, those proportions are probably already there, quietly doing their work.

16: The Rhythm of Work

THERE'S A RHYTHM to good turning that goes beyond technique. It's the pace at which you move, the way you sequence operations, the balance between action and pause[37]. When you find this rhythm, the work flows. When you fight it, everything feels forced.

I notice this most clearly when teaching groups. In a workshop with five lathes running, each person develops their own tempo. Some rush, making cut after cut without pausing to assess. Others move so slowly that momentum never builds. The best work comes from those who find their natural pace: steady, considered, but not hesitant.

This rhythm isn't the same for everyone. Some people think faster and work faster. Others need more time to process. Neither is better. What matters is finding your authentic pace and working within it rather than trying to match someone else's tempo or meet some imagined standard of speed.

When I first started turning, I was impatient. I wanted to finish pieces quickly, to see results, to move on to the next thing. This rushing created problems. Catches from pushing too hard. Surfaces that needed excessive sanding because I hadn't cut cleanly. Proportions felt wrong because I hadn't taken the time to assess them.

Gradually, I learnt to slow down. Not dramatically, but just enough to breathe between cuts, to step back and look, to let my hands rest briefly before the next pass. This small shift changed a lot. The work became more enjoyable. The results improved. I wasn't working slower in terms of total time; I was working more efficiently by reducing errors.

There's also rhythm within each operation. The way you move the tool has tempo: steady, smooth, controlled. Jerky movements produce jerky surfaces. Smooth movements produce smooth surfaces. Your body learns this rhythm through practice, and eventually it becomes automatic.

I can hear rhythm in other turners' work. The sound of the lathe, the sound of the cut, the pauses between passes. These create an audible rhythm that tells you something about the maker's process. Experienced turners have a steady, almost musical quality to their work. Beginners sound chaotic, arrhythmic[38].

Listen for it sometime. An experienced turner's workshop sounds almost like percussion. The steady hum of the lathe, then the smooth whoosh of a cut, a brief pause, another cut. The tempo is consistent. The pauses are deliberate. There's a pattern you could almost tap your foot to. A beginner's workshop sounds different: erratic starts and stops, long silences followed by frantic activity, the stuttering sound of catches and corrections. The difference is audible before you even see the work.

This isn't about speed. Some of the best turners I know work quite slowly. Others work quickly. What they share is consistency of rhythm. There are no frantic sections or dead stops. The work progresses at whatever pace suits the maker, but that pace is maintained steadily.

Rhythm also applies to how you sequence operations. There's a logical order to most turning projects: roughing, shaping, refining, detailing, sanding, finishing. Rushing through the early stages to get to the finishing creates problems. Spending too long on refinement when the form isn't yet resolved wastes time. Finding the right sequence and spending appropriate time on each stage is part of establishing good rhythm.

There's also the rhythm of a session. Some days I work for hours, deeply focused. Other days I can only sustain attention for shorter periods. Learning to recognise and respect these natural rhythms prevents forcing work when I'm not present. Better to stop and return later than to push through and make mistakes from fatigue or distraction.

Physical rhythm matters too. The way you stand, shift weight, move your body as you work. All of this has rhythm. Tense, rigid posture disrupts rhythm. Relaxed, flowing movement supports it. I've watched beginners freeze in place, gripping tools tightly, barely breathing. Experienced turners move with their work, shifting position naturally, breathing easily.

Watch an experienced turner's body sometime. Their weight shifts smoothly from foot to foot as the tool travels along the piece. Their shoulders stay relaxed, dropping away from their ears. Their grip on the tool is firm but not tight enough to be strangling the handle. They might step slightly to the left as they work toward the headstock, then shift right as they move toward the tailstock. The whole body is involved in the work, not just the hands. Some people call it the woodturner's dance.

This body awareness develops slowly. At first, you're so focused on the tool and wood that you don't notice your physical state. Eventually, you feel the tension, the held breath, the locked joints. Once you notice these patterns, you can soften them. The work becomes less physically demanding and more rhythmically fluid.

Music and rhythm have interesting parallels. Musicians practice to develop consistent tempo. They learn when to pause, when to accelerate, when to sustain and follow the notes on their sheet music. Turners need similar skills. The cuts have tempo. The sessions have structure. The projects have pacing. All of this is rhythm in different scales.

I occasionally listen to music while turning, and I notice my work pace tends to match the music's [39]tempo. Fast music, faster work. Slow music, more contemplative pace.

This isn't necessarily good or bad, but it's worth noticing. If rhythm affects your work, you can use it deliberately by choosing music that supports the pace you want, rather than letting it determine the pace unconsciously.

There's also the rhythm of the year. In winter, I tend to work differently than summer. Shorter days, colder workshop, different light. These environmental factors may affect your rhythm. Rather than fighting them, I work with them, accepting that winter work might be slower, more focused, while summer work might be more expansive, experimental.

Professional turners develop strong work rhythms because production demands it. You can't make a living if you spend all day on one piece. But rushing reduces quality. The challenge is finding a sustainable pace that maintains quality while producing adequate quantity. This is where good rhythm becomes essential. It maximises efficiency without sacrificing craftsmanship.

I've noticed that my best work happens when I'm neither rushing nor dawdling. There's a pace where I'm moving steadily but have time to observe, to respond, to adjust. Too fast and I miss information. Too slow and I overthink. The sweet spot is somewhere in between, and it feels like rhythm when I find it.

This optimal rhythm changes with experience. Early on, everything takes longer because you're figuring things out. As skills develop, natural pace quickens because you're not pausing to remember what comes next. But it should never become mechanical. Even with deep familiarity, there should be space within the rhythm for observation and response.

Teaching has taught me about rhythm too. I have to match my teaching pace to students' learning pace. Too fast and they feel overwhelmed. Too slow and they lose interest. Finding the right instructional rhythm requires attention to the group, reading their body language, their engagement, their confusion or confidence.

Different projects demand different rhythms. A large vessel might require sustained focus over hours or days. A small detail piece might be complete in thirty minutes. Learning to shift rhythms between projects is part of versatility. You're not locked into one pace; you adapt to what the work requires.

There are also cultural rhythms worth considering. Some making traditions value speed and efficiency. Others value contemplation and deliberation. Neither is wrong, but they produce different relationships with work. I lean toward the contemplative end of the spectrum, but I appreciate makers who work with different rhythms. There isn't one right way.

Rhythm also relates to breath. When you're working well, you breathe easily and naturally. When something is wrong, when you're tense or forcing something, your breath becomes shallow or stops entirely. Noticing breath is a quick way to check rhythm. If breath is constricted, pace needs adjustment.

What specifically makes experienced turners different? They never reach for a tool they don't need. They don't make cuts twice when once would do. They never stop to figure out what comes next because they already know. Each movement flows into the next without hesitation. When there is a pause, it is deliberate, to assess, to plan. When they move, it is decisive. There is no wasted energy anywhere in the process. That's what good rhythm looks like when it's fully developed.

This is what I aim for. Not speed, but flow. Work that moves steadily through operations without friction or forcing. Rhythm that feels natural rather than imposed. Pace that matches my energy and attention rather than some external standard. When I find this rhythm, time passes without notice. Hours feel like minutes. The work is effortless not because it's easy but because it's flowing.

So when students ask how long something should take, I tell them it takes as long as it takes. The question isn't speed but rhythm. Find your natural pace. Work within it. Let the rhythm emerge from attention to the work rather than imposing it from outside. This is how craft becomes practice, not by rushing to finish, but by settling into sustainable rhythm that can be maintained over years.

17: Patience Under Pressure

RUSHING CREATES PROBLEMS. Patience solves them. This is one of the fundamental truths of making, and one I've had to relearn repeatedly. When deadlines loom or enthusiasm peaks, the temptation to hurry is strong. But wood doesn't respect urgency. It responds to care.

We've all seen it happen, I'm sure. A piece left until the last moment, rushed to meet a deadline. The wood doesn't cooperate. A catch tears the surface. Aggressive sanding to fix it creates new scratches. Moving through grits too quickly leaves those scratches visible. By the time finish goes on, the surface tells the story of every shortcut taken. Each rushed decision makes the next problem worse. The cascade of impatience is almost always the same, and the result is a piece that looks exactly like what it is: hurried.

Patience is particularly difficult when things go wrong. A catch ruins a surface you'd nearly perfected. A crack appears in the wood you thought was stable. A measurement error means starting over. These moments test patience more than the routine work does. The temptation is to rush the repair, to force a solution. But rushing a fix usually makes things worse.

I've learnt to pause when problems arise[40]. Step back. Breathe. Assess calmly. What actually happened? What are the options? What's the best approach rather than the fastest? This pause creates space for patience to operate. Without it, reaction dominates, usually poorly.

Patience under pressure also means maintaining standards when it would be easier to compromise. When time is short, the temptation is to accept good enough rather than holding out for actually good. Sometimes good enough truly is sufficient. But often it's an excuse for impatience dressed up as pragmatism.

I try to ask myself: will I be satisfied with this compromise tomorrow? Next week? Next year? If the answer is no, better to take the extra time now than live with regret later. This long-term thinking helps resist the short-term pressure to finish quickly.

Patience is also required for repetitive tasks. Sanding through multiple grits. Applying multiple coats of finish. Making multiple identical pieces. These tasks can be tedious, and the temptation to rush or skip steps is strong. But the cumulative effect of patience, working thoroughly through each stage, produces results that rushing can never match.

There are also moments of forced patience: waiting for a wood delivery, waiting for tools to arrive, waiting for workshop repairs. These delays are frustrating because they're external. But they, too, are opportunities if approached with patience. Time to plan. Time to practice. Time to learn something new. Resistance makes delays worse; acceptance makes them useful.

Pressure can come from within too. Personal deadlines. Self-imposed standards. The desire to prove something to yourself or others. This internal pressure can be more intense than external deadlines because you can't negotiate with yourself as easily. Patience here means being realistic about what's achievable and being willing to adjust expectations when circumstances demand it.

I've made the mistake of pushing through illness, through fatigue, and through distraction because I set a goal and felt obligated to meet it. The work produced during these sessions is rarely good. Better to acknowledge the reality, adjust the timeline, and return when conditions are better. This isn't a weakness. It's wisdom.

Patience also requires trust. Trust that taking time will

pay off. Trust that working carefully produces better results than working quickly. Trust that skills build reliably through practice, even when progress feels slow. Without this trust, pressure dominates. You feel you must force results because you doubt they'll come naturally.

I develop this trust by tracking progress over time. Looking at early work compared to recent work. Noticing improvements that happened so gradually I didn't see them happening. This evidence of growth reinforces trust in the process, which supports patience under pressure.

There's also communal pressure. When working alongside others who work quickly, the temptation to match their pace is strong. But everyone has different experience levels, different natural tempos, different standards. Patience means working at your pace rather than someone else's, even when comparison is uncomfortable.

Patience is also required when success comes slowly. You make piece after piece that doesn't quite work. The breakthrough you're seeking stays elusive. Progress feels minimal. This is when pressure builds: to abandon the project, to lower standards, to conclude you can't do it. Patience means continuing despite slow progress, trusting that breakthroughs happen through accumulated effort even when they're not immediately visible.

I remember spending months trying to teach myself the cut needed to turn the inside of a bowl. Piece after piece was scratched out with poor technique and sanded to death. I couldn't articulate why, but something was off. Most pieces went in the scrap bin. The pressure to give up and just use a scraper to finish it off was significant. I was wasting time and wood on failure. But I trusted the process. Eventually, something clicked. I saw what had been wrong. The piece was a zebrano bowl, about ten inches wide, and what made it especially gratifying was that I sold the piece about a week later.

The problem was tool presentation and how the gouge needed to move smoothly. The bevel was off the wood and creating terrible tool marks. I was teaching myself at the time as I couldn't afford lessons. It seems obvious now, but it took dozens of failed attempts before it clicked in my head to draw the handle back towards me a bit to engage the bevel on the wood. That breakthrough only came through patient persistence, through making enough wrong bowls that the right answer eventually became visible.

Patience under pressure also means knowing when to stop for the day. When fatigue or frustration builds, patience wears thin. Continuing past this point produces poor work and increases risk of an accident. Better to stop, rest, and return fresh. This requires overriding the pressure to finish now, trusting that tomorrow will be more productive than forcing through today.

There's humility in patience. It acknowledges that you don't control all variables. Wood has its own nature. Skills develop on their own timeline. Results emerge when conditions are right. You can influence these things but not command them. Patience is accepting this limited control rather than fighting it.

I think about this in terms of farming versus manufacturing[41]. Manufacturing demands control: exact specifications, precise timing, predictable results. Making is more like farming. You plant, tend, nurture, and wait for growth. You can't force crops to mature faster. You work with natural rhythms. Patience is essential. Learning to turn is farming, not manufacturing.

So when pressure builds, from deadlines, from expectations, from ambition, remember that good work requires patience. Rushing might produce something finished, but it rarely produces something excellent. Patience might feel like an indulgence when pressure is high. But it's actually the most practical approach because it produces better results with fewer problems. The pressure will always be there. Learning to work patiently despite it is what separates work you'll be proud of from work you'll regret.

18: The Final Touch

THE LAST FIVE percent of a piece takes as much attention as the first ninety-five percent[42]. Finishing is where respect for your craft shows most clearly. You can turn a beautiful form, but if you rush the sanding or apply finish carelessly, all that work is diminished. The piece becomes ninety-five percent excellent and five percent careless, and that five percent is what people will notice.

I've seen this countless times. The turner is clearly excited to be nearly done, eager to see the finished piece, so they sanded it quickly, missing scratches or creating uneven surfaces. They then apply the finish without checking dust or preparing properly. The piece is almost right, which somehow makes it more disappointing than if it were wholly wrong. Almost is the most frustrating place to stop.

Finishing well requires deliberately slowing down when every instinct wants to speed up. The piece is right there, nearly complete. You can see what it will become. The temptation to rush these final steps is enormous. But the finish reveals everything you may have missed. Every tool mark and scratch, every area you under-sanded. Every bit of dust you failed to remove. The finish doesn't hide mistakes. It illuminates them.

One piece springs to mind. It was a piece of cedar of Lebanon, about 20 inches across. After turning and sanding it down, I was going through the finishing process for it. I had opted for a simple oil finish. I find large pieces become overpowering if the finish is over-complicated. Anyway, I was applying some oil to the back of it, when I noticed a scratch in the surface. As it was on the underside of the platter, I nearly ignored it as it would hardly ever be seen. Then though, I thought that I'd be letting myself, and the piece down if I didn't correct what I could see was wrong. So I remounted the piece, sanded it back (after the oil had cured) and finished it properly. I felt better that now everything was right with the piece, I wouldn't look at it knowing that I hadn't corrected the scratch.

It didn't take long, and compared to the lifespan of the piece, it is no time at all.

Surface preparation is crucial and perhaps more complex than it appears[43]. You're not just smoothing wood. You're progressively removing the marks left by each previous step. Coarse sandpaper removes tool marks but leaves its own scratches. Fine sandpaper removes those scratches but leaves finer ones. The progression continues through the grits until the scratches are too small to see. Skip a grit and the coarse scratches may remain visible under your finish no matter how much you sand with finer paper.

The standard progression is 120, 180, 240, 320, 400 grit for most work. Some pieces benefit from going finer: 600 or even 800 grit for very smooth finishes. But each additional grit has diminishing returns. The difference between 320 and 400 is noticeable. The difference between 600 and 800 is subtle. Learn to recognise when enough is enough. I rarely sand lower (higher?) than 400 as if I can't see any surface marks, I'm not sure if going further is actually worth it.

I teach students to look and feel between grits. When the lathe has stopped, run your hand over the surface. Can you feel scratches? If yes, continue with that grit. Look at the surface from different angles. Can you see scratches? If yes, continue. Only move to the next grit when the current one has done its job completely. Patience here prevents problems later.

Sanding technique matters as much as grit selection. Most people sand too hard, pressing the paper into the wood with force. This doesn't speed the process. It just heats up the wood and clogs the paper. Light pressure with movement is more effective. Let the abrasive do the work. Your job is to move it consistently over the surface, not to press it in with strength.

Light pressure lets the abrasive do the work. If your arm is tired after a few minutes, you're pressing too hard.

Dust removal is equally important and frequently neglected. Sanding dust settles into pores and grain. If you apply finish over this dust, it becomes locked in place, creating a muddy appearance instead of clarity. I use compressed air to blow surfaces clean after sanding, followed by a tack cloth to pick up remaining dust. This seems fussy until you see the difference it makes.

The space between sanding and finishing is critical. Don't rush from one to the other. Let the piece rest for a moment. Look at it in a different light. Check for areas you might have missed. Run your hands over surfaces again. This pause catches problems while they can still be fixed. Once the finish is applied, opportunities for correction become much more limited.

Your choice of finish depends on both your use and aesthetic goals for the piece. Oil finishes enhance grain and feel wonderful but provide minimal protection. They're appropriate for decorative pieces or items that won't see hard use. Lacquer protects well but can look plastic if applied poorly. Wax feels luxurious but requires reapplication and offers little protection. Understanding these trade-offs helps match finish to purpose.

I tend toward natural finishes: oils, waxes, simple approaches that let the wood speak[44]. I do love a satin lacquer, though! I'm not dogmatic. Some pieces benefit from more robust finishes. A salad bowl needs food-safe protection that will survive washing. A decorative vessel can prioritise appearance. The key is choosing consciously based on the piece's intended life rather than defaulting to whatever is convenient.

I also find its size is important to the choice of finish, too. Too big, and a super-glossy finish becomes overpowering. All you can see is your own reflection, as if you're in a hall of mirrors. Tone it down to a satin, or flat finish, and the results will be far more understated and impressive.

Application technique matters tremendously. Oil applied too thickly creates sticky buildup that never fully dries. Wax buffed too aggressively creates heat that melts it away rather than bonding it to the wood. Lacquer applied in humid conditions can blush, developing a cloudy white appearance. Every finish has requirements. Understanding and respecting them determines results.

I prefer multiple thin coats over single thick coats for any liquid finish. Thin coats dry faster, penetrate better, and build depth gradually. Thick coats sag, take forever to dry, and often create application problems. This requires patience: waiting between coats, resisting the urge to apply more than the surface can absorb. But the results justify the time. A well-finished piece has depth that thick coats can't achieve.

Applying finish to wood that's too wet traps moisture, leading to problems months later. Applying finish to wood that's too dry can result in poor penetration. Understanding moisture content and finish requirements prevents these issues. Personally, I like to work with wood between 10% and 14% moisture content.

Finishing is also where detail work shows or fails. A cleanly turned foot gets noticed and appreciated. A rough or unfinished bottom suggests carelessness that undermines the entire piece. Small transitions between elements, where a rim meets a body, where a base meets a foot, these details reveal whether you cared about the whole piece or just the obvious parts.

I remember being taught to finish the bottom of pieces as carefully as the visible surfaces. At first this seemed excessive. Who looks at the bottom? But people do look (particularly woodturners!). They pick up pieces, turn them over, assess them completely. A rough bottom tells them you didn't finish the work. A smooth, considered bottom tells them you cared about the entire piece. That difference matters.

There's satisfaction in finishing well that goes beyond the visual. It's the knowledge that you cared enough to do every step properly. That you respected your own work enough to see it through completely. That you honoured the material and the craft by doing your best throughout, not just at the impressive stages. This integrity shows in the final piece and in your own relationship with the work.

I think about how pieces will be experienced. Most people won't know how difficult the turning was or what challenges you overcame. But everyone can feel a smooth surface. Everyone notices good finish. Everyone responds to details done well. Finishing is how your care becomes tangible to others. It's your last communication with the person who will live with this piece.

This is particularly true for gifts or commissioned work. These pieces carry extra responsibility. Someone is receiving your work as a representation of your skill and care. Finishing well honours that trust. It says: I made this for you with full attention. Every aspect has been considered. Nothing was left to chance or rushed through.

Even for pieces you keep yourself, finishing matters. Living with something poorly finished is a constant reminder of impatience or carelessness. Every time you see it or use it, you notice what you didn't do. Living with something well finished is a quiet pleasure every time you encounter it. The piece finished well rewards you repeatedly. The piece finished poorly reproaches you constantly.

There's also professional consideration if you hope to sell work. Finishing quality directly affects perceived value. Two pieces with identical forms but different finishing will sell for different prices or at different speeds. The well-finished piece looks more valuable because the finishing demonstrates care. People are buying craftsmanship, and finishing is where craftsmanship is most visible to non-makers.

I've learnt not to make excuses for poor finishing. Not to say it looks better in person, or the scratches aren't really noticeable, or I was rushing to meet a deadline. These excuses don't change the reality that the finishing was rushed. Better to acknowledge the truth: this piece wasn't finished as well as it could have been. Then commit to doing better next time.

Finishing is where perfectionism and pragmatism must balance. Pursuing perfect finishing can prevent you from ever completing anything. The goal isn't perfection but excellence: doing everything as well as is reasonable given time, tools, and circumstances.

I aim for finishing that looks deliberate. Clean transitions. Consistent surfaces. Thoughtful finish choice. Attention to details. When these elements align, the piece feels finished. A piece that feels finished in all respects, that requires nothing more, that represents your best work at this moment.

So when I talk about finishing well, I'm talking about respecting the entire process. Not phoning it in at the end because you're tired or excited. Not rushing because you can see the goal. Taking the time to do the final five percent with the same care you gave the first ninety-five percent. That integrity shows. People might not articulate why one piece feels better than another, but they feel it. The difference is finishing, and finishing is everything.

Learning the nuances and technicalities of turning the inside of a bowl. 2024.

Part Four

What the Work Means

Making changes you. This chapter examines that transformation: how form emerges through the act of making rather than before it, how we learn to recognise completion, how skill becomes embodied memory, how solitude and community each serve the maker, how control and release work together, and how simplicity often says more than complexity. These aren't techniques but ways of understanding what you're doing and why it matters.

19: A Shape Emerges

DESIGN DOESN'T HAPPEN only at the drawing stage. It happens throughout the making process, in response to what the wood reveals, what your hands discover, what emerges through dialogue between your ability, your intention and the material. But that dialogue needs a strong starting point. Without a clear design to guide you, the conversation can become aimless at the lathe.

I work from sketches and diagrams almost exclusively. They're not optional for me. They're how I think through a piece before I commit to cutting wood, how I test proportions on paper where mistakes cost nothing, and how I ensure the shape I want to achieve is clear in my mind before the lathe starts turning. A good sketch is a discipline. It stops you from drifting into vague approximations of what you meant to make.

And here's the thing: the sketch needs defending.

Wood has opinions. Grain runs unexpectedly. Knots appear where you didn't want them. The blank suggests one thing when you'd planned another. It's tempting to follow where the material leads, to let the wood "speak to you" and guide you toward something different from your original intention. Sometimes that's appropriate. More often, it's a way of losing your nerve. Wood cannot speak to you as such, but it can suggest what it could be. Look carefully at it, and see if you can design a shape that will preserve that lovely piece of figure, of the knot in it[45]. If not, don't worry about it.

Proportions are fragile. A form that works beautifully on paper can fall apart if you drift too far from it during execution. The gentle curve you planned becomes too full. The delicate stem thickens because the wood was fighting you and you compensated. The foot grows heavier than it should because you were nervous about stability. Each small departure seems reasonable in the moment, but they accumulate. By the end, you've made something that resembles your design but doesn't embody it. The proportions that made the sketch work have been compromised by a dozen tiny surrenders, possibly because you are nervous to leave your comfortable zone of ability and confidence!

Your sketch represents the thinking you did when you weren't under pressure, when you could consider the whole form and how its elements relate. At the lathe, with wood spinning and tools in hand, it's easy to lose that overview. You're focused on the immediate cut, the surface right in front of you. The sketch holds the bigger picture so you don't have to keep it all in your head while you're working.

I'm not saying you should ignore the wood entirely. Material has properties that matter, and fighting them completely is foolish. If the grain is tearing badly in one direction, you adjust your approach. If a flaw appears that genuinely can't be worked around, you respond. But there's a difference between sensible adaptation and abandoning your design because the making got difficult. The former is craft. The latter is drift.

I remember one student who came to a workshop with a candlestick design he'd drawn carefully beforehand. This was unusual for him. He'd told me he rarely worked from sketches, preferring to let shapes emerge as he turned. His previous work showed it: pleasant enough pieces, but vague, lacking the clarity that comes from deliberate proportion.

But this time he had a drawing. Proper measurements. Considered relationships between the base, the stem, the candle holder. He'd thought it through.

At the lathe, he stuck to it. When the wood pushed back, he pushed back harder. When cuts didn't go cleanly, he refined his technique rather than changing the shape. When he was tempted to thicken the stem because it felt precarious, he checked his sketch, saw the proportion he'd planned, and trusted his earlier thinking over his present anxiety. A good sketch can help with your confidence if you are feeling wary.

The finished candlestick was the best piece he'd made. Not because the design was revolutionary, but because he'd actually realised it. The proportions he'd considered on paper were there in the wood, intact, not eroded by a series of expedient compromises. He could see what he'd intended, fully embodied. That's a different experience from looking at something and thinking "well, it's close to what I wanted."

He told me afterwards that having the sketch changed everything. It gave him something to defend, a standard to hold himself to. Without it, every decision was negotiable. With it, he knew when he was drifting and could correct.

This is what design discipline provides: a reference point that exists outside the pressures of the moment. When you're tired, when the cut is difficult, when the wood is being awkward, your judgement in the moment isn't always reliable. The sketch is reliable. It represents your clearest thinking about what this piece should be. Trusting it over your momentary impulses usually produces better work.

There's also the question of what happens when you don't have a design. Some turners pride themselves on working spontaneously, letting forms emerge through intuition rather than planning. I understand the appeal. It feels creative, responsive, free from constraint. But watch what they actually produce. Often it's clunky shapes, heavy feeling pieces, 'almost there' vases, repeated with minor variations, because without deliberate design, you default to what your hands already know. Intuition isn't infinite. It's a library of familiar moves. Design pushes you beyond the familiar.

I tend to design for long-term satisfaction rather than immediate impact. I want pieces that reward living with, that reveal their qualities slowly, that you appreciate more after a year than you did in the first week. This means simple forms, good proportions, attention to tactile qualities, surfaces that invite touch or simply just to look at from the sofa. These characteristics develop value over time while flashy elements can become tiresome. This long-term thinking influences every design decision, often toward simplicity and away from elaboration. But simplicity requires precision. Simple forms expose every proportion. There's nowhere to hide when the shape is plain. This is why simple designs need the most careful execution, the most disciplined adherence to what you planned.

Design through making also involves editing, but editing within a framework. As the piece develops, you might see opportunities to simplify, to remove elements that don't serve the whole, to clarify your intention. This subtraction can be valuable. But it should be deliberate rather than expedient. Removing a detail because you've reconsidered its contribution to the whole is different from removing it because you couldn't execute it cleanly. The first is design refinement. The second is retreat dressed up as choice.

I remember making a vessel that had multiple decorative bands in the original sketch. As I worked, I reconsidered. One band was enough. More was excessive, cluttered, distracting from the form rather than enhancing it. I removed the extra elements and the piece was stronger for it. But I made that decision from a position of capability, not limitation. I could have made the additional bands. I chose not to. That's editing. If I'd abandoned them because they were too difficult, that would have been something else entirely.

This distinction matters. When you're learning, it's easy to confuse the two. You tell yourself you're making a design choice when really you're avoiding a challenge. Honest self-assessment helps here. Ask yourself: am I changing this because I've genuinely reconsidered, or because I'm finding it hard? If the answer is the latter, consider whether you should push through rather than around.

There's also the matter of responding to genuine accidents. Sometimes things happen that your design couldn't anticipate. A crack develops. A catch tears the surface. A flaw appears that changes everything. These moments require real response, not rigid insistence on the original plan.

I once had a bowl crack partway through turning. My first reaction was disappointment. Wasted wood, wasted time, failed piece. But looking at the crack, I saw it could become a feature rather than a flaw.

Understanding your own aesthetic helps with all of this. What forms satisfy you? What proportions genuinely feel right? What details matter to your eye? These preferences develop through making many pieces and paying attention to which ones you love and which ones you merely tolerate. Your personal aesthetic emerges from accumulated experience, from noticing patterns in your responses to your own work and to others'.

I notice patterns in my making. Forms I return to, proportions I prefer, curves that feel natural under my hands. I tend toward forms that embody graceful curves and crisp transitions. I prefer feet that are proportional and suit the piece rather than oversized or too delicate, depending on the intended purpose of the piece. I'm drawn to clean forms where colour or texture, if used, support the wood's natural figure. I didn't decide these preferences consciously. I discovered them by looking at years of work and noticing what I kept returning to, what still pleased me long after the making was finished.

These preferences inform my designs. But they don't replace the need to design deliberately for each piece. Knowing I prefer proportional feet doesn't tell me exactly how they should be for this particular form with these particular proportions. That requires specific thinking, sketched out and considered before I start cutting. The preferences give me a starting vocabulary. The design applies that vocabulary to the specific piece I'm designing.

There's also cultural influence on what we find beautiful. The forms we consider pleasing are partly personal and partly shaped by what we grew up seeing, what our visual environment taught us to appreciate. Being aware of these influences doesn't negate them, but it helps distinguish between what you truly prefer and what you've absorbed without examination. This awareness allows more intentional choices.

I draw inspiration from many sources: pottery, architecture, natural forms, historical turning, different cultures, and the work of makers I admire. But inspiration is different from copying. Inspiration is seeing a curve relationship in a piece of ceramics and thinking about how that might translate to wood. Copying is trying to reproduce someone else's piece exactly. Inspiration enriches your design vocabulary and expands what you think is possible. Copying replaces your voice with someone else's. The difference is intention. Are you learning from the work, or avoiding the harder task of developing your own eye?

Design through making is ultimately about maintaining intention under pressure. The lathe is spinning, the tool is cutting, things are happening quickly. It's easy to lose sight of what you meant to make. The sketch keeps you anchored. It represents thinking you did carefully, without time pressure, considering the whole. Trust it over your moment-

20: Knowing When to Stop

KNOWING WHEN TO stop cutting and start finishing is one of the hardest skills to develop. The temptation to make one more adjustment, to refine just a bit further, to chase perfect symmetry: these impulses can lead you past the point of optimal form into territory where you're weakening rather than improving.

I've ruined pieces by not stopping. A finial that was elegant lost its top half because I refined it too aggressively. A thin-walled bowl shattered with 'just one last cut'. In each case, I knew I should stop but pushed anyway, driven by some misguided idea of what perfect meant or misreading the signs the piece was giving me.

The wood will tell you when it's done. The form will feel right. The proportions will balance. The surface will be ready for finishing. Learning to recognise that moment, and to honour it by stopping. This requires trust in your judgement and resistance to the seductive idea that more work (or "one more cut") always equals better results.

There's a concept in many making traditions called wabi-sabi: the appreciation of imperfection. Knowing when that irregularity is character versus when it's sloppiness is part of knowing when to stop.

I've found that the moment when a piece feels done and the moment when I'm tempted to continue are often the same moment. The piece is good. I'm satisfied. But there's always the thought: what if I could make it just a little bit better? This is where discipline matters. Recognising that good is good enough, that pursuing perfect can and does occasionally lead to worse.

This applies to wall thickness particularly. Thin walls impress people. There's satisfaction in turning something delicate. But there's also risk. Go too thin and the piece loses structural integrity or even shatters. It becomes anxious to look at rather than pleasing. Knowing when thin enough is thin enough requires experience and honesty about whether you're serving the piece or serving your ego. A decent sketch here will help with proportions.

How do you judge when you've reached the right thickness? Part of it is feel. As walls get thinner, they start to vibrate differently under the tool. There's a point where that vibration feels alive and responsive. Go past it, and the vibration becomes nervous, unstable. The tool starts to chatter because there's not enough material to support the cut. That's your warning.

I've learnt to ask myself: am I continuing because the piece needs it or because I want to prove something? If the answer is the latter, it's probably time to stop. Proof of skill should come from appropriate execution, not from pushing beyond what the piece requires.

Knowing when to stop also means recognising when a piece has failed beyond recovery. Some mistakes can't be fixed. Some wood has flaws that make the planned form impossible. Continuing to work on something that can't succeed is waste disguised as persistence. Better to admit failure early and move on than to invest more time in something doomed. Or, redesign on the fly and see how it turns out. If it fails, it's no problem as the original piece had failed anyway, but you tried. If it genuinely succeeds, then great! That's a win for you.

There's humility in knowing when to stop. It acknowledges that you don't have unlimited time, unlimited wood, or unlimited energy. Choices must be made. Not every piece will be your best work. Some will be good enough, and that's acceptable. Perfection isn't achievable;

excellence is. Knowing the difference prevents both underwork and overwork[46].

Stopping at the right time also relates to knowing your own fatigue. When you're fresh, judgement is good. As fatigue builds, judgement deteriorates. Continuing past your effective working time produces poor decisions and poor work. Better to stop for the day and return fresh than to push through and make mistakes from tiredness.

I've ruined more pieces from working tired than from almost any other cause. The signs are obvious in hindsight: impatience, sloppiness, catches from inattention. But in the moment, fatigue clouds judgement. Learning to recognise your own signs of declining performance and stopping before damage occurs takes experience and honesty[47].

I have a box of almost-finished pieces. Mostly they are pieces made in demonstrations or lessons, and are seldom as good as I want them to be. Maybe someday they'll call me back. Maybe not. Either way, they served their purpose by getting me far enough to teach something, even if they didn't reach completion.

Knowing when to stop with design is particularly important. You can endlessly refine proportions, adjust curves, modify details. At some point, these refinements cease to improve the piece and become procrastination disguised as perfectionism. The design is good enough to execute. Further planning delays making. Time to commit and begin.

I sometimes get this paralysis when I plan extensively but never start. I'm always refining the design, always finding one more thing to adjust. Planning feels productive and safe. Making is risky. But I'll learn more from making one imperfect piece than from perfecting plans for a dozen pieces never made. Perhaps I ought to re-read Lesson One again!

Stopping also means being willing to complete pieces that

aren't your best work. Not everything will be extraordinary. Some pieces are practice. Some are experiments. Some are just okay. Finishing these pieces, even though they're not exceptional, builds finishing skills and prevents the perfectionist trap of only working on pieces you think might be perfect.

There's also practical consideration. If you never finish anything because you're always refining, you have no completed work. Completion matters. A finished piece, even if imperfect, has more value than ten partially complete perfect pieces. Stopping and finishing is how you build a body of work rather than a shop full of almosts.

I try to give each piece the attention it deserves. No more, no less. A quick project doesn't need the same refinement as a major piece. Matching investment to purpose prevents both underwork and overwork. This calibration, knowing how much is enough for this particular piece, develops through experience.

The ability to stop at the right time also relates to confidence. You have to trust that good is good, that this piece succeeds at what it was meant to do, that pursuing hypothetical improvement risks actual deterioration. That confidence comes from completing many pieces and seeing that the ones you stopped at good were often better than the ones you pushed to perfect.

So when I feel that tug to continue, to make one more pass, to refine one more detail, to thin the walls just a bit more, I need to pause. I should ask: does this piece need more work, or do I need to prove something? Is this improvement or anxiety? If I'm working from anxiety rather than from the piece's actual needs, it's time to stop. Trust that what's done is done well enough, and move on to what comes next.

I've also learnt through experience that the right stopping point varies with the piece. A practice piece where efficiency matters has a different threshold than a once-in-a-lifetime commission piece. Knowing which standard applies and working to it rather than to some abstract ideal of perfection is part of mature judgement.

What does this look like practically? A practice piece might stop at 320 grit and a simple oil finish. It needs to be good, but it also needs to be efficient. Spending an extra hour on each piece when you're practising is perhaps not really worthwhile. A commission piece will certainly go up to 400 grit, get multiple coats of a carefully applied finish, have every detail attended to meticulously. The client is paying for that care. Once you've figured out the technique you were exploring, further refinement teaches nothing new. Different purposes, different stopping points. The mistake is applying exhibition standards to practice work, or practice standards to commissions.

There's also physical stopping, when your body tells you to stop. Fatigue makes judgement poor and mistakes more likely. Continuing past your effective working time produces poor decisions that create more work later.

So knowing when to stop isn't a weakness or a compromise. It's wisdom. It's recognising that work done well enough is actually done. The pursuit of theoretical perfection often makes work worse rather than better. That your initial instinct about completion is often correct and second-guessing creates problems. Trust that moment when the piece feels complete. Stop. Move forward to what comes next.

21: The Hands Remember

YOUR HANDS KNOW more than your mind thinks they do. After enough practice, they develop memory that operates below conscious [48]thought. This 'muscle memory' (body knowledge) is one of the great gifts of repetitive craft work. It frees your mind for higher-level thinking while your hands manage the technical work.

I notice this most when demonstrating. I can talk about the piece, its design, answer questions, engage with the audience or students, all while my hands continue turning. They know where the tool needs to be, how much pressure to apply, when to adjust. This automaticity only comes through practice, through letting the body learn through repetition. I'm obviously keeping an eye on what they are doing, but most of my concentration is on communicating verbally what I am doing.

Trusting your hands means not overthinking every movement. There's a point where analysis becomes paralysis, where thinking too much interferes with doing. Once you've practiced enough, sometimes the best approach is to let your hands lead and your mind follow (but only when you are comfortable and experienced enough that this feels natural!). They often know the way even when your conscious mind is uncertain.

This doesn't mean working mindlessly. Your hands are acting on accumulated knowledge, not random movement. Every cut they make without conscious direction is informed by thousands of previous cuts. The learning is there. It has just moved from conscious thought to automatic action.

I remember when this shift happened for me. For months, every cut required conscious attention. Tool angle, pressure, direction: all deliberate decisions. Then gradually, my hands started making these adjustments automatically. I'd realise halfway through a cut that I wasn't thinking about technique. I was thinking about form while my hands handled execution.

The transition feels strange at first. You become aware that your hands have been working 'without you', like waking from a daydream to find you've driven several miles without conscious memory of the journey. There's a moment of alarm: was that okay? Then you look at the surface and it's fine. Better than fine, actually. Smoother than when you were consciously controlling every movement. That's when you start to trust it. Not blind trust, but earned trust based on evidence that your hands know what they're doing. (A quick note here, it really is not a good idea to drive several miles without paying attention! The point I am making here is that auto-pilot in the head exists and ought to be kept in check!)

This transition is uncomfortable. You have to trust that your hands will do the right thing with minimal oversight. Early attempts to relax conscious control often lead to mistakes because automaticity isn't yet reliable. But pushing through this awkward phase is how you get to genuine fluency.

Different operations require different levels of conscious attention. Roughing cuts, once learnt, can be largely automatic. Delicate finishing cuts require more conscious involvement even with experience. Knowing which operations can be trusted to body memory and which require full attention prevents both overthinking and carelessness.

I've also learnt that fatigue affects this trust. When I'm fresh, my hands are reliable. As tiredness builds, automatic

This is different from being stuck in a habit. You can try new tools, new techniques, new approaches. But after a fair trial, if your hands prefer certain methods, that preference deserves respect. You're not being close-minded. You're working with your actual physical reality rather than fighting it to match some theoretical ideal.

Trusting hands also means trusting them to rest. They know when they need pause, through slight tremor, through loss of precision, through discomfort. Ignoring these signals and pushing through leads to poor work or injury. Your hands are giving you information. Trust them enough to stop when they indicate they need rest.

I used to power through hand fatigue. Now I view it as information. Tired hands make mistakes. Taking breaks to rest your hands isn't an indulgence. It's pragmatism. Fresh hands work better than tired ones. Trusting this and acting on it improves both work quality and long-term hand health.

There's also tactile trust. Your hands feel things you can't see: vibration, resistance, temperature, texture. These tactile inputs provide constant feedback about what's happening at the cutting edge. Trusting this feedback rather than depending entirely on visual information makes you a better turner.

I sometimes demonstrate this by asking students to focus on what they can feel and hear, rather than what they can see. Keep your eyes open, but shift your attention to what the tool and wood are telling you. Notice the vibration travelling up the tool. Listen to the changing pitch as the cut deepens or lightens. Feel the moment the bevel finds its riding point, or whether you are pulling or pushing the tool into the wood rather than finding the cut.

Most people are surprised by how much information is already there, waiting to be noticed. We rely so heavily on vision that we forget our hands are constantly gathering data. The difference between a clean cut and a dig-in often announces itself through feel before it ever becomes visible. Learning to trust that feedback, to let the hands lead while the eyes confirm, is one of the quiet shifts that marks a developing turner.

This doesn't mean ignoring vision. It means integrating tactile and visual information rather than depending primarily on visual. When hands and eyes agree, you have confirmation. When they disagree, something needs attention. Both sources of information matter, but many turners under-utilise tactile feedback by over-trusting vision.

Trusting hands also involves trusting intuition about form. Your hands holding the piece give you information about weight, balance, how it sits in the palm. This physical interaction with the piece provides design feedback that looking can't. A form might look good but feel wrong when handled. Trusting that feeling and adjusting based on it improves work.

Over time, I've learnt to trust my hands' first instinct about cuts. The initial movement is usually right. It's informed by all that accumulated experience[49]. Conscious interference often makes things worse, second-guessing what the body already knows. This doesn't mean never adjusting, but it means respecting what hands want to do as a starting point.

This trust is hard-won. It requires practice to build competence, attention to develop awareness, patience to let automaticity develop, and courage to act on body knowledge even when the conscious mind is uncertain. But once established, this trust transforms turning from a conscious struggle into a flow of information between the mind and the hands where both contribute their particular forms of knowledge.

Body memory isn't mystical. It's neurological[50]. With enough repetition, motor patterns become encoded in ways that don't require conscious processing. This frees-up cognitive resources for higher-level decision-making. Your hands manage the tool presentation while your mind thinks about form and proportion. This division of labour is essential for complex work. Without it, you'd be overwhelmed trying to consciously manage everything simultaneously.

I notice this most clearly when tired. When fresh, my hands perform reliably even while my conscious mind is partially elsewhere. As fatigue builds, automatic competence decreases and I must consciously direct more of what my hands do. This increased cognitive load is exhausting and why work quality declines with tiredness. The automatic systems become less automatic, requiring conscious attention that drains limited mental resources.

There's also trust that develops through crisis. When something goes wrong (a catch, a tear, an unexpected problem) do your hands know how to respond? In those moments, there's no time for conscious thought. Your hands must act on accumulated knowledge immediately. This crisis competence only develops through experiencing and recovering from many problems. Each recovery teaches your hands something about emergency response.

Trusting your hands ultimately means trusting the process of learning through repeated doing. Your hands won't suddenly know things they haven't practiced. But give them consistent, attentive practice over time, and they develop capabilities that conscious thought can't match. This body knowledge is one of craft's great gifts. It turns complex sequences of movements into fluent action, freeing your mind for creative thought while your hands manage execution. That's the promise of trusting your hands. Not that they'll magically know things, but that through practice they'll develop knowledge that serves you reliably.

22: The Company We Keep

MUCH OF MY turning happens in solitude. Just me, the lathe, and whatever piece of wood I'm working with. Hours pass without conversation, without interruption, without another person's presence in the workshop. This solitude isn't loneliness. It's something I've come to value deeply, a necessary condition for the kind of focused attention that good work requires. This is how I prefer to work on pieces I'm turning for the first time.

There's a quality to working alone that can't be replicated when others are present[51]. Your attention is undivided. You're not performing, not explaining, not aware of being watched. You can make mistakes without embarrassment, try things that might not work, have conversations with yourself about what you're seeing and feeling. The work becomes intimate in a way that's difficult when you're conscious of an audience, even a friendly one.

I notice the difference immediately when someone enters the workshop while I'm turning. Part of my attention shifts to them, even if they're just watching quietly. I become slightly more careful, slightly more conventional, slightly less willing to experiment. The work doesn't suffer dramatically, but something changes. The deep absorption that produces my best work requires solitude. I can't fully lose myself in the process while remaining aware of another person's presence.

But there's a different mode too, once the form is established and the work becomes more rhythmic. This is how I like to finalise shapes and decorations. My hands know the moves, and I can relax a bit, and the company in the workshop is an encouragement rather than a distraction.

This solitude also provides space for thinking that has nothing to do with turning. The hands are busy, the conscious mind is occupied with the work, and somewhere underneath, other processing happens. Problems I've been struggling with find resolution. Ideas emerge that seem unconnected to what I'm doing. Emotions that I've been avoiding surface and can be felt without the distraction of conversation or obligation. The workshop becomes a place for more than making. It becomes a place for being alone with yourself in ways that modern life rarely permits.

I've come to protect this solitude as often as possible. I don't answer the phone while turning. I keep the workshop door locked so visitors don't casually wander in. I schedule teaching and collaborative work for specific times, preserving other times for solitary practice. This is recognition that my solitude serves purposes that company can't, and that both have value.

But solitude has limits. Working entirely alone, you only ever encounter your own ideas, your own solutions, your own mistakes[52]. You develop habits without knowing they're habits because you've never seen anyone do it differently. Your understanding becomes deep but narrow, shaped entirely by your particular experience. Growth slows because you've exhausted what you can discover independently.

This is where community becomes essential. Watching another turner work, even for an hour, can reveal approaches you'd never have discovered alone. Their solutions to problems you share, their different relationship with tools and material, their aesthetic choices that differ from yours: all of this expands what you thought was possible. You return to your own workshop with new questions, new experiments to try, new awareness of assumptions you didn't know you were making.

I remember visiting a turner whose workshop was organised completely differently from mine. Tools I kept at the lathe, he kept across the room, walking to them when needed. I thought this was inefficient until I watched him work. Those walks gave him pause, moments to look at the piece from a distance, time to consider before the next cut. What looked like poor organisation was actually built-in reflection. I didn't adopt his layout, but I did start stepping back more deliberately, building pauses into my own workflow. That insight came from watching someone else, from being in his space rather than my own.

Demonstrations and symposiums serve this purpose on a larger scale. Watching many turners work, seeing the variety of approaches to similar challenges, absorbing different philosophies of making: this concentrated exposure accelerates learning in ways that solitary practice can't match. Even in my own club, Woodturning360 and the monthly demonstrations we have from some of the worlds best demonstrators, I always return from these events energised, full of things to try. The community refreshes what solitude can make stale.

There's also the value of conversation about the work, separate from the doing of it. Discussing pieces with other makers, hearing how they think about form and material and process, articulating your own thinking in response: this verbal exchange deepens understanding in different ways than physical practice. Some things become clear only when you try to explain them. Some questions only arise when someone else asks them. The community of conversation complements the solitude of making.

A student once asked me why I pause briefly before starting a finishing cut on a bowl's interior. I hadn't realised I did this. But when I paid attention, I found the pause was real, a moment where I reset my grip, confirmed the tool angle before committing to a cut that would be visible in the finished piece. I'd developed this habit unconsciously over years, and it took a student's observation to make it visible to me. That understanding came from teaching, not from practice.

Students also bring fresh perspectives that challenge settled thinking. They ask why about things I stopped questioning years ago. They struggle with things I find easy, forcing me to understand those things more deeply in order to help. The best teaching sessions leave me learning as much about teaching as the students learn about turning.

Collaboration on actual pieces is rarer in turning than in some crafts, but it happens. Working with another maker on a shared project requires negotiation, compromise, communication that solitary work doesn't demand. You can't just follow your instincts. You have to articulate them, defend them, sometimes abandon them in favour of someone else's better idea. This can be uncomfortable but productive. The piece that emerges is different from what either maker would have produced alone, sometimes better, always instructive about your own tendencies and blind spots.

There's also the informal community of makers you never meet but whose work you encounter. Pieces in galleries, images online, work at exhibitions: these silent conversations with other makers shape your understanding of what's possible. You see a form you'd never considered, a surface treatment you didn't know existed, a proportion that challenges your assumptions about what works. These encounters with work rather than workers still constitute community, still pull you beyond the limits of solitary discovery.

The online world has expanded this dramatically. I can watch a turner in Japan work through a technique and in the next minute, I can see what makers in America, Australia, Scandinavia are exploring. This global visibility means that contribute as well as things to learn. The relationship with community has matured along with the work.

I've found my own rhythm with this. Mostly solitary practice, punctuated by teaching, by visits to clubs, by events and watching demonstrations, by conversations with makers I respect. The solitude provides depth. The community provides breadth. Neither alone is sufficient. The work needs both the quiet hours of focused making and the energising contact with others who share the practice.

What I value most, perhaps, is returning to solitude after community. Coming back to my own workshop after watching others work, after conversations about making, after the stimulation of different approaches. The solitary practice is enriched by what I've encountered. The quiet hours have new questions to explore, new experiments to try. The dialogue between alone and together continues, each mode feeding the other, neither complete without its complement.

The workshop door closes. The lathe starts. I'm alone again with the work. But I'm not isolated. Everything I've learnt from others is present in how I approach the next piece on the lathe. The community is here even in solitude, accumulated in my practice, shaping work that will eventually go back out into the world to inspire others I'll never meet. Working alone, I'm still working together. The solitude contains multitudes.

23: Control and Release

THERE'S A PARADOX at the heart of turning. You need control to work safely and effectively, of course, but too much control creates rigidity. The best work comes from a balance: enough control to guide the tool, enough release to let the work flow[53].

I struggled with this when I was getting started. Early on, I held tools tightly, moved rigidly and tried to force outcomes. The work felt stiff and my body would sometimes ache from tension. Gradually, I learnt to relax my grip, to let the tool rest more lightly, to guide rather than force. The work improved immediately and became far less tiring.

This balance between control and release extends beyond physical technique. It applies to design too. You need enough structure to work with enough freedom to respond to what emerges. Plans guide but perhaps should not dominate. Control serves the work; it should not constrict it.

Control comes from technique: knowing how to present your tools, understanding grain direction, and having reliable methods. This technical foundation provides safety and capability. But control exercised too rigidly can prevent adaptation. The wood doesn't always behave exactly as predicted. The form wants to go slightly differently than planned. Rigid control fights these variations. Balanced control accommodates them within reason.

I think of control as a container, rather than a cage. It provides boundaries within which work happens but doesn't dictate every detail. A piece needs certain structural requirements: a stable base, an attractive form, and appropriate wall thickness. These are containers. Within them, many variations are possible. Control establishes the container; release explores within it.

Release doesn't mean abandoning standards or working carelessly. It means loosening unnecessary tension in grip, expectations, and attachment to specific outcomes. Tight grip transmits every minor tremor to the tool. Relaxed grip absorbs variation, producing smoother cuts. Tight expectations make every deviation feel like failure. Relaxed expectations permit discoveries.

I notice this in students constantly. Beginners grip tools desperately, as if holding tighter increases control when in fact it does the opposite. Tension creates rigidity that amplifies problems. Teaching them to soften their grip feels counter intuitive to them. They fear loss of control. But softening the grip can actually improve control by allowing responsive adjustment rather than rigid forcing.

The same applies to body position. Overly tense, locked posture feels controlling but is actually limiting. Taking a relaxed, mobile stance allows your body to move with the work, adjusting position fluidly. This responsive positioning is true control: the ability to adapt instantly. Rigid positioning is false control, the appearance of stability masking inability to adjust.

There's also breath. Holding breath creates whole-body tension[54]. Breathing easily maintains relaxation while working. I catch myself holding my breath during delicate cuts, instinctively trying to control everything. But holding my breath reduces oxygen, increases tension, and actually decreases capability. Breathing through challenging moments maintains the relaxation that enables control.

Release also applies to mistakes. Tight attachment to perfection makes every error feel catastrophic. Relaxed acceptance that mistakes happen allows you to address them calmly. The error is just information to enable you adapt and continue. Tension around mistakes often creates more mistakes as anxiety interferes with capability. It can end up as a vicious circle if you're not careful.

I've learnt that my best work happens when I'm working hard but feeling easy. The effort is there: attention, precision, care. But the feeling is relaxed. This combination produces control with flexibility. I'm guiding work toward goals but remaining open to where it actually wants to go. One more element that helps with working but feeling easy is the use of the design of the piece I am working on. By having a scale drawing to hand means I don't have to worry about trying to control the tools *and* create a shape I have in my mind - It's there in front of me and is therefore one less thing for me to think about.

What does this state actually feel like? My shoulders are down, not creeping up toward my ears. My jaw is relaxed, not clenched. I'm breathing steadily without thinking about it. My grip on the tool is firm enough to direct it but loose enough that I could wiggle my fingers if I wanted to. There's focus without strain. I'm aware of what's happening at the cutting edge but not fixated on it. Time passes without me noticing. If someone asked how I was feeling mid-cut, I'd say something like "fine" or "good" rather than "tense" or "concentrating hard." The effort is real but it doesn't feel like effort.

This balance shifts with fatigue. When fresh, I can maintain relaxed control for hours. As tiredness builds, maintaining balance becomes harder. I either tighten up in compensation, trying to force continued capability, or I become too loose, losing precision. Recognising when fatigue has disrupted balance and stopping before quality deteriorates is important.

There's also emotional release needed. Attachment to outcomes creates tension. This piece must be perfect. This technique must work. These absolute demands interfere with process. Releasing attachment doesn't mean not caring.

It means caring about doing good work without demanding specific results. The process becomes the focus; outcomes become byproducts.

I find this easier with practice pieces than with important projects. With practice, I can explore freely because failure has no consequences. With important work, stakes feel higher, tension increases, control tightens. Learning to bring the practice mindset to important work mentally, and to maintain that exploratory freedom even when outcomes matter, is an ongoing challenge.

Control and release also interact with tool sharpness. Sharp tools require less pressure, allowing relaxed control. Dull tools require forcing, which increases tension and decreases control. Maintaining sharp tools is partly about enabling this relaxed control, working with tools that cooperate rather than resist.

There's also the question of ego. Much excessive control comes from ego: proving ability, demonstrating skill, forcing outcomes that display competence. This ego-driven control creates tension and often produces worse work than releasing ego-attachment and just working. The piece becomes about the work itself rather than what the work proves.

I notice this when teaching. I can demonstrate more freely than when trying to prove something because demonstration is about the technique, not about me. When ego is engaged, when I'm wanting to impress or needing to succeed, control tightens, and performance often suffers. Releasing ego-attachment paradoxically improves capability.

Balance between control and release is ultimately about trust. Trust in the fact that you have sufficient skill. Trust that appropriate control is enough. Trust that releasing unnecessary tension won't lead to chaos. This trust builds through experience, through seeing that relaxed control produces better results than tense control. Evidence accumulates that loosening up works, which makes loosening up easier.

So when you work now, check periodically: where am I holding tension unnecessarily? Where am I controlling more than I need to? Can I soften, release, let this work flow more easily? These small adjustments often produce immediate improvement. The work becomes less effortful, more enjoyable, and often better as control and release find their balance.

There's also control versus force. Control is directing energy efficiently. Force is overwhelming resistance with power. They feel different. Control is smooth, directed, purposeful. Force is tense, rigid, and inefficient. Beginners often confuse the two, thinking more pressure equals more control. It does the opposite. More pressure usually means less control because you're fighting rather than guiding.

I demonstrate this with a simple exercise. Hold a tool with death-grip tension. Now try to make subtle adjustments to the angle or position. It's difficult because the tension locks everything in place. Now, relax the grip significantly. Suddenly, subtle movements become easy. You have more control with less effort because you're not fighting your own tension.

Students are often surprised by this. They loosen their grip and expect the tool to feel unstable, uncontrolled. Instead, it feels more responsive. They can make tiny adjustments they couldn't make before. They can feel the wood's feedback more clearly because tension isn't drowning out the subtle signals. That's the paradox. Releasing unnecessary control gives you more real control.

This seems counterintuitive but it's fundamental to all skilled movement.

Release also applies to outcomes. Attachment to specific results creates anxiety that interferes with process. If this piece must be perfect or I have failed, then every small imperfection becomes catastrophic. If this piece is an exploration and whatever results is learning, then imperfections are just information. The piece is the same either way, but your relationship with it changes how you work on it.

This doesn't mean not caring about results. It means caring more about the process than the outcomes[55]. Focus on doing each step well rather than on the final result. Paradoxically, this focus on the process often produces better results than focus on the outcome because you're fully present with the work rather than anxious about the future. Your attention is where it's useful, on what you're doing now, rather than where it isn't, on what might happen later.

I've made my best work when I cared deeply about doing good work but was detached from whether any particular piece succeeded. This combination of care and release is difficult to maintain but extraordinarily productive when achieved. You're working as well as you can without the weight of must-succeed pressuring every decision. That freedom allows risk-taking and experimentation that tight outcome-focus prevents.

Control and release must dance together. Too much control and you can't adapt. Too much release and you lose direction. The sweet spot is having enough structure that you know what you're working toward but enough flexibility that you can respond to what actually happens rather than forcing predetermined outcomes. This balance isn't static. It shifts with experience, with fatigue, with the particular challenges of each piece. Learning to find it and maintain it is ongoing work, but it transforms turning from struggle into flow.

Control and release also shift with the phase of work. Roughing out requires more forceful control because you're removing material quickly. Finishing requires more release to-moment impulses. Defend the proportions you planned. Fight for the form you envisioned.

The wood will have opinions. Some of them are worth hearing. Most of them are just resistance to be worked through. Learning to tell the difference is part of developing as a maker. But when in doubt, trust your design. It knows things your anxious hands might forget.

So when I teach design, I encourage students to learn to draw with intention. Consider proportions carefully. Think through how elements relate before you start cutting. Then hold onto what you've planned. Don't let difficulties erode it. Don't let the wood talk you out of your own thinking. Make the piece you designed, not an approximation of it softened by a hundred small compromises.

The best pieces aren't happy accidents. They're clear intentions, carefully held, fully realised in wood.

movements become less precise. Continuing to trust hands that are no longer trustworthy leads to mistakes. Recognising when fatigue has compromised automatic competence and stopping for rest is part of mature practice.

Trusting your hands also means accepting their limitations. They can't do what they haven't practiced. If you attempt a new technique, conscious attention is required until body memory develops. Expecting automaticity where no automatic knowledge exists is misplaced trust. You have to earn trust through practice specific to each skill.

I see students struggle with this. They want their hands to know things their hands haven't learnt yet. When automatic competence doesn't materialise, they conclude they lack talent. But talent isn't the issue. Practice is. Part of learning is through repetition. Give your hands that repetition and they'll become trustworthy.

I've had to unlearn several poor habits over the years. My grip was too tight. My stance was too rigid. The tool angle to the wood needed tweaking. Each correction required conscious attention to override automatic patterns. Eventually, better patterns became automatic, but the transition was effortful. Starting correctly would have been easier.

For years, I'd been self-teaching with the tool at what I thought was the right angle. It wasn't, as I found out when I finally took a lesson with Les Thorne. Changing it was harder than learning it in the first place. My hands had spent years encoding the wrong default. It took several pieces of conscious correction before the new angle felt like home.

Trusting your hands also extends to tool selection. Your hands develop preferences: tools that feel right, grips that work well, angles that are comfortable. Trusting these preferences rather than second-guessing them leads to better work. Your hands are telling you what works for your body. Listen.

good ideas spread faster than ever, and that isolation is a choice rather than a circumstance. But it also means that influence can become homogenising, everyone watching the same videos, absorbing the same approaches. The local and personal can get lost in the global and popular. I try to balance online exposure with direct contact. The screen shows much but transmits little of the tactile reality that defines our craft.

The balance between solitude and community shifts over time. Early in development, community matters enormously. You need exposure to possibilities, correction of errors, models of what good work looks like. You learn faster with guidance than without it. As skills develop, solitude becomes more valuable. You need time to integrate what you've learnt, to develop your own voice rather than imitating others, to go deep rather than constantly encountering new surfaces. Later still, the balance shifts again. Teaching, (for me at least) becomes important, both for what it gives others and for what it reveals to you. Community becomes less about learning and more about contributing, about playing your part in the tradition's continuation.

When I started turning, I sought out every video I could to watch others work as I was not in a position to afford lessons and short on time to visit clubs. I was hungry for input, aware of how much I didn't know, eager to absorb everything I could. That was right for that stage. Later, I pulled back, spent more time alone in the workshop, worked through what I'd gathered. Too much input was becoming noise rather than signal and far too many influences to find a single technique I should adopt. I needed to find my own approach within everything I'd absorbed. Now, years further on, I find myself seeking community again, but differently. Less as a student, more as a participant in an ongoing conversation. I have things to because you need sensitivity to subtle feedback. Moving between these modes within a single session requires flexibility, adjusting control and release as the work demands.

Here's what that shift looks like practically. When roughing a bowl, I'm taking aggressive cuts, removing material efficiently. My grip is firmer, my stance more planted, my movements more deliberate. I'm in control of the process, directing it forcefully. As I move to refining the shape, I lighten up. Cuts become lighter, grip loosens, I start paying more attention to what the wood is telling me. By the time I'm making finishing passes, I'm barely there. The lightest touch, the most relaxed grip, maximum sensitivity to feedback. I'm not controlling the cut so much as allowing it to happen while staying present to guide if needed. These are different modes, and shifting between them fluidly within a single piece is part of mature turning.

There's also learning when to let pieces go. Some projects become struggles where control and release both fail to produce satisfying work. Knowing when to abandon a piece rather than fighting it to completion is wisdom. Not every blank becomes something worth keeping. Not every start deserves finishing. Releasing attachment to completion and accepting that some work serves only as learning is mature judgement.

24: Less, but Better

THE IMPULSE TO add another detail, another flourish, another element, is often strong. But simplicity often communicates more effectively than complexity[56]. A clean curve, a balanced proportion, a surface that needs no embellishment: these can be more powerful than decorated elaboration.

I remember making boxes for a craft fair once. The first few were simple, with clean lines, good proportions, and natural finishes. Then I got bored and started adding decorative bands, carved lids, and coloured details. I thought I was improving them. The customers thought otherwise. The simple boxes sold immediately. The decorated ones sat largely unsold. The message from that fair was clear.

Looking back, I can see what went wrong. The decorative bands competed with the wood's natural figure rather than complementing it. The carved lids, while technically accomplished, made the boxes feel fussy rather than refined. The coloured details dated the pieces, tying them to a particular moment rather than letting them feel timeless. Each addition was meant to make the boxes more interesting. Instead, each addition made them less coherent. The simple boxes worked because everything in them served a purpose. The decorated boxes failed because the additions served my ego rather than the design.

This isn't an argument against decoration or complexity. Both have their place. But they should be deliberate choices that serve the design, the season, and even the marketplace where you may be selling, not defaults that mask weak form. Sometimes the bravest design choice is to do less, to let the material and proportion speak without embellishment.

Simplicity is harder than it appears. With complex work, individual elements can hide weaknesses. With simple work, everything shows. The curve must be perfect. The proportions must balance. The surface must be flawless. There's nowhere to hide poor execution. This is why simple work is actually more demanding than complex work. It requires better fundamentals.

I've noticed that as my skills have improved, my work has largely become simpler. Early pieces were busy, with lots of details, multiple elements, decorative features. I was showing what I could do. Later pieces are quiet, with clean forms, subtle curves, and careful proportions. I'm showing what the wood can be. The focus shifted from maker to material, and simplicity followed naturally.

This mirrors what I see in many craft traditions. Student work is elaborate. Masterful work is more simple[57]. The students are demonstrating capability. The masters are demonstrating understanding. They know that form and proportion carry meaning more effectively than decoration. Their confidence allows restraint.

Simplicity also ages better. Trendy details date quickly. Clean forms stay relevant. A simple vase made fifty years ago looks timeless. An elaborately decorated bowl made five years ago looks dated. If you're making objects meant to last, simplicity serves that longevity better than complex styling tied to particular aesthetic moments.

There's also functional consideration. Simple forms are easier to clean, easier to store, easier to use. Complexity for its own sake often compromises practicality. A simple lidded box functions as well as a complex one but causes fewer frustrations. Sometimes the best design is the one that gets out of its own way.

I'm not arguing for boring plainness or my pet phrase of 'round and brown'. Simple doesn't mean simplistic. A simple form can have extraordinary presence: subtle curves that reward extended viewing, proportions that feel inevitably right, surfaces that invite touch. This richness comes from refinement, not from accumulation of elements.

The challenge is developing an eye for what's essential. What does this piece actually need? What can be removed without loss? Often, the answer is most things can be removed. The essential core (a good curve, a balanced proportion, a considered foot) carries the design. Everything else is optional, and often better left out.

I practice this through editing. Start with more, remove elements until the piece begins to suffer, then add back that last element. What remains is the minimum necessary, the essential form without excess. This subtractive approach often produces better results than additive design where you keep adding until it feels complete.

Here's what that looks like in practice. I was making a piece for my first book 'Woodturning Form and Formula', and my initial sketch had a decorative band around the shoulder, a textured foot, and a slightly flared rim. I made it as sketched. It looked busy. So I removed the textured foot, just made it plain. Better, but still not right. I removed the decorative band. Now the form could 'breathe'. In the end I binned it from the final collection as I decided to settle with more simple forms with minimal additions.

Simplicity also respects the material. Highly figured wood doesn't necessarily need decorative enhancement unless the whole piece will benefit from it. Its own patterns provide visual interest. Plain wood might benefit from surface treatment, but figured wood may be better left simple so its natural beauty shows. Matching design simplicity to material character prevents competing for attention.

There's confidence required for simplicity. Complex work can hide behind its complexity. The busyness distracts from weaknesses. Simple work has nothing to hide behind. Every proportion, every transition, every curve is visible and must stand on its own merit. This exposure is why simple work feels vulnerable to make.

But that vulnerability is also honesty. Simple work says: this is what it is, no pretence, no distraction. That honesty communicates integrity. People respond to it even if they can't articulate why. A simple piece done well feels trustworthy in a way elaborate work often doesn't.

There's also the question of making time. Simple forms can be made well more quickly than complex forms. If you're making for sale, this matters economically. But it also matters philosophically. Simplicity allows focus on quality of execution rather than quantity of elements. Better to make one excellent simple piece than one adequate complex piece.

Simplicity forces you to get the details absolutely right. With complex work, small errors get lost in overall piece. With simple work, small errors are glaring. This demanding standard actually improves your work across all forms. Learning to execute simple forms excellently makes you better at everything else.

What kind of errors become visible? A curve that's almost smooth but has a flat spot. A foot that's slightly too wide. A rim that may be proportionally too thin or wide. A transition between wall and base that's abrupt rather than flowing. In a busy, decorated piece, these flaws disappear into the visual noise. In a simple piece, they're the only things to look at. You can't hide them, so you have to fix them. That discipline, learnt through simple work, carries over into everything you make.

I think about Japanese aesthetic principles: wabi-sabi valuing imperfect simplicity, ma valuing negative space, shibui valuing understated elegance[58]. These principles evolved through centuries of consideration about what makes objects satisfying to live with. The consistent conclusion: simplicity aged well, complexity often didn't.

This doesn't mean copying Japanese aesthetics. Every culture has simple forms worth studying. Shaker furniture, Scandinavian design, traditional pottery across cultures: all show that simplicity is a universal quality that transcends particular traditions[59]. It speaks to something fundamental about how humans perceive and value objects.

So when I begin to design and make a piece now, I think about how little I can add rather than how much. What's the simplest form that achieves the goal? What elements are truly necessary versus optional? This minimalist thinking produces work that feels calm and confident rather than busy and anxious. The pieces are quieter but often more powerful because nothing distracts from their essential nature.

Simplicity also serves accessibility. Complex work with multiple elements, elaborate detail, and busy surfaces can be impressive but also overwhelming or alienating. Simple work invites engagement. People can understand it, appreciate it, feel comfortable with it. This doesn't mean simple work is less sophisticated. Often it's more sophisticated because it requires deeper understanding to know what to include and what to omit.

I'm not arguing that everyone should make simple work. Complex and highly decorative pieces have their place and their pleasures. Some makers thrive on elaboration and some work demands it. But I've discovered since my deep dive into mathematical proportions that simplicity is undervalued, particularly by beginners who confuse complexity with skill. Some think they must add elements to demonstrate capability. Often the opposite is true. Simplicity demonstrates a confidence and understanding that complexity can overpower.

There's practical consideration too. Simple forms are easier to execute cleanly than complex ones. This doesn't make them easy. Clean execution of simple work is quite difficult. But you're dealing with fewer variables, fewer opportunities for error. This means more pieces succeed, less wood is wasted, less time is spent fighting problems. If you make your living from turning, this practical advantage matters economically.

Choosing simplicity also means accepting limitation. You're choosing to work within constrained vocabulary, to explore depth rather than breadth, to find interest through refinement rather than addition. This self-imposed limitation is creative constraint that focuses exploration. When you can't add elements endlessly, you must make each element essential. That pressure produces thoughtful work.

So when I advocate for simplicity, I'm advocating for thoughtfulness, intentional choices and about what matters for the benefit of the piece. For the confidence to leave well enough alone rather than constantly adding. For trust that good form and proportion carry their own power without requiring decoration to make them interesting. Simplicity isn't easier. It's harder because that difficulty produces work that rewards extended attention, that remains satisfying over time, that feels inevitable rather than arbitrary. That's the beauty of simplicity.

Working with cameras has become part of the job.
Tool shop demonstration, 2019.

Part Five

What Remains

Every maker eventually asks: what lasts? This final chapter considers legacy in its many forms: how time adds value to honest work, how teaching transforms both teacher and student, how learning never actually ends, how making can become meditation, how curiosity sustains a lifetime of practice, and how we each participate in something larger than ourselves. The circle of craft has no beginning and no end. We join it for a while, contribute what we can, and pass it on.

25: The Patina of Time

HOW A PIECE ages matters as much as how it looks when new. Wood changes over time. Colours deepen, surfaces develop character, and use leaves marks. These changes aren't flaws. They're part of the piece's life story.

I love seeing old work of mine after years in people's homes. A salad bowl with slight discolouration in the bottom from decades of dressing. A box with wear marks at the lid edge from constant opening and closing. A vessel whose finish has deepened to warmth that new work can't have. These pieces have lived. They've become part of people's daily lives rather than remaining separate objects. That integration is a success beyond anything technical.

When I'm making now, I wonder about this future life. Will this piece age gracefully? Will wear enhance it or reveal poor making? Will it survive decades of use? Will the finish develop character or just look worn? These considerations influence everything from wood selection to surface treatments. I'm not just making for now. I'm making for decades hence.

Different woods age differently. Cherry darkens dramatically from pale pink to rich brown[60], sometimes within just a few months of exposure to light. Maple barely changes, staying close to its original pale colour for decades. Oak develops golden warmth, its open grain collecting dust and grime that deepen its character. Walnut, which starts dark, actually lightens slightly over time, the deep chocolate mellowing to warmer brown. Yew develops extraordinary depth, the contrast between heartwood and sapwood becoming more pronounced. Understanding these aging characteristics helps choose wood appropriate to the piece's intended life. If you want dramatic change, choose cherry. If you want stability, choose maple. If you want a piece that will look completely different in twenty years than it does today, plan for that transformation. Or don't overthink it, and just make something.

Finishes also age. Oil darkens slightly over years, deepening in colour and developing richer tones. Wax needs occasional renewal but maintains its character well with proper care. Lacquer can yellow over time, particularly in sunlight. These aren't problems if anticipated and incorporated into expectations. The finish is part of the piece's evolution, not a permanent state. Understanding these aging characteristics helps you choose finishes appropriate to how you want pieces to evolve.

There's a Japanese concept of mottainai: regret over waste, respect for things and their lifecycles[61]. Objects aren't disposable. They're partners in daily life, changing and aging alongside their owners. This perspective values patina as evidence of life lived together rather than as deterioration to be avoided.

I now try to design pieces that will age well, that wear will enhance rather than diminish. This means good design that will survive use or as an ornamental piece. Finishes that deepen and age well (in my opinion). Forms simple enough that they don't date. These considerations make pieces that improve with time rather than deteriorate.

What does robust construction actually mean? Walls thick enough to withstand decades of handling without becoming fragile. Feet substantial enough that they won't chip or wear through. Joints designed with wood movement in mind so they don't crack as humidity changes across seasons and years. These aren't visible features. No one will notice them in the finished piece. But they're the difference between a bowl that's still in use in fifty years and one that cracked, chipped, or wore through decades earlier.

A bowl used daily develops wear patterns that tell stories about its life. Slight stains where fruit sat too long. Faint marks from careless handling. These marks aren't damage, but rather the piece's biography. They transform the piece from a pristine object to a lived companion. This transformation requires both durability to survive use and acceptance that use changes things.

This perspective also affects what I make. Disposable work, pieces meant to be briefly enjoyed then discarded, holds no interest for me. I want to make things that last, that become better through use, that people will keep and eventually pass through the family as an heirloom. This requires making well enough to survive decades of living.

I think about pieces I've inherited: old tools, family objects, things made by hands now gone. What do they communicate about their makers? What will my work communicate about me to people I'll never meet? Someone decades from now might encounter a piece I made in an antique shop or estate sale, long after I'm gone. They won't know me or the circumstances of its making. But they'll respond to the object itself: its form, its surface, its character developed through time. Will it speak well of its maker? Will it demonstrate care and skill? Will it justify the resources consumed in its creation?

This long view encourages integrity. You can't fake quality across decades. Only genuine care endures. Creating work that communicates across time requires attention to timeless qualities: good proportion, honest material, careful execution.

Patina also teaches humility. Your perfect finish will age. Your crisp details will soften. The pristine piece you complete will accumulate marks of use. Accepting this is part of letting go of control and trusting in time. The piece's life extends far beyond the moment you finish it, and much of that life will happen without you.

There's beauty in this ageing. A well-used candlestick that shows its history honestly is more interesting than a perfect unused one. The patina tells stories: dinners served, hands that held it, years it participated in daily life. This narrative quality develops only through time and use. New work can't have it, no matter how well-made.

The patina of time also includes the maker's evolving relationship with their own work. Pieces I was proud of when new sometimes disappoint years later as my standards rise. Pieces I was uncertain about when new sometimes become favourites as I understand them better. This shifting assessment is natural. You change, your understanding deepens, and your perspective broadens. The work stays the same, but your relationship with it evolves. Time is the ultimate judge, revealing what endures and what was merely fashionable.

There's also collective patina, how work from a period or place ages together. Certain approaches or finishes characteristic of a time become markers of that time. Future viewers will see not just individual pieces but patterns across many makers working in similar ways. Your work contributes to that collective record. Being aware of this encourages choices that will represent your moment well to future viewers.

Patina creates authentication too. In an age of mass production and perfect replication, wear and aging prove authenticity. The uneven patina of genuine use can't be faked convincingly. A piece that shows honest wear from decades of living tells truth about its age and origins that pristine objects can't. This truth-telling quality makes aged objects trustworthy in ways new objects aren't.

I also notice that pieces age differently depending on their environment. A bowl in daily kitchen use develops different character than one displayed on a shelf. A box handled frequently ages differently than one touched rarely. These different aging patterns tell stories about how pieces lived. Understanding this helps you anticipate how choices about construction and finishing will affect how pieces age in their likely environments.

So when I finish a piece, I try to imagine it twenty years hence. How will it have changed? What marks will it carry? Will it still feel satisfying, or will it look dated? These questions help me make choices that serve long-term rather than immediate appeal. Because ultimately, pieces live far longer than the moments of their creation. And there's humility in knowing your work will outlast you, that unknown hands will hold what you made, that objects carry makers forward into time we'll never see.

26: The Next Revolution

TEACHING CLARIFIES UNDERSTANDING. When you explain something to someone else, you discover what you truly know[62] versus what you only think you know. This is why teaching has been so valuable to my own development. It forces precision in thinking and honesty about limitations.

I remember the first time a student asked me why we hold the bowl gouge at a particular angle. I'd been doing it automatically for years, but I'd never articulated why. Trying to explain forced me to understand the mechanics: how the angle affects the cut, why it matters, what happens when you adjust it. I found myself drawing diagrams, demonstrating the difference between angles, watching the student's face for the moment of understanding.

What I discovered in trying to explain it was this: the angle determines which part of the edge is cutting, and that determines whether fibres are sliced cleanly or torn. Too steep and you're scraping rather than cutting. Too shallow and the edge digs in rather than gliding. The sweet spot presents just enough edge to slice while the bevel supports the cut. I'd known this in my hands for years. I'd never put it into words. That student taught me something I thought I already knew.

Student questions expose assumptions you didn't realise you were making, areas where your understanding is more intuitive than explicit. Someone asks why we cut in a particular direction, and suddenly you're thinking through grain orientation in ways you'd stopped consciously considering years ago. Someone struggles with a technique you find easy, and you have to break it down into components you'd long since merged into single movements. Articulating why something works the way it does forces deeper understanding. Teaching is therefore a continuation of learning, not separate from it.

Passing knowledge on isn't just generosity. It's also growth. Every question challenges your understanding. Every different learning style requires you to find new ways to explain. Every student's struggle reminds you how difficult things were when you were learning, how much you've internalised that once required conscious effort. Teaching keeps you humble and keeps you learning. It prevents the complacency that can settle in when you work alone, unchallenged by fresh perspectives.

There's also satisfaction in watching someone grasp something you've explained. That moment when understanding clicks, when confusion transforms to clarity, is one of the great pleasures of teaching. You can see it happen: the furrowed brow relaxes, the tentative movements become confident, the questions shift from "how" to "what if." You've helped someone move forward. Knowledge that lived only in you now lives in them too, to be developed and eventually (hopefully) passed on again. That multiplication of understanding across people and time is deeply satisfying in ways that solitary mastery can't match.

There's also the question of what deserves passing on. Techniques are obvious: how to sharpen, how to cut, how to finish. These mechanical skills can be demonstrated, practiced, and refined. But attitudes and approaches matter equally. How do you relate to materials? How do you respond to mistakes? How do you balance planning with adaptation? How do you know when a piece is finished? How do you maintain standards when no one is watching? These philosophical elements shape how techniques are applied. They determine whether someone becomes a maker who respects their craft or merely someone who can operate tools. Passing on techniques without this context produces technically capable makers who lack the deeper understanding that makes work meaningful.

The philosopher Michael Polanyi explored this distinction in his influential work "The Tacit Dimension"[63] (1966), coining the phrase "we can know more than we can tell." He was describing what he called *tacit knowledge*: the understanding that resides in skilled practice but resists explicit articulation. You can write instructions for sharpening a gouge, but the feel of when it's truly sharp, the subtle resistance that tells you the edge is right, that knowledge lives in the hands and can only be acquired through practice. Polanyi argued that this tacit dimension underlies all skilled activity, from riding a bicycle to recognising faces to, yes, turning wood on a lathe.

This has profound implications for craft teaching. Researchers studying apprenticeship have found that only about 20-30% of the knowledge in skilled practice can be made explicit through documentation and instruction[64]. The remaining 70-80% is tacit: absorbed through observation, imitation, and guided practice within what scholars call a "community of practice." This is why traditional apprenticeships lasted years, not weeks. It's why watching someone work, even without verbal instruction, transfers knowledge that words alone cannot fully convey.

I think about this when I'm teaching. The explicit knowledge is the easy part: tool angles, cutting sequences, safety procedures. I can write these down, demonstrate them clearly, test whether students have understood. But the tacit knowledge, the stuff that actually makes the difference between competent work and excellent work, requires something different. It requires time together at the lathe.

This is why I believe the attitudes deserve as much

attention as the techniques. Patience, respect for materials, curiosity about problems, acceptance of mistakes: these aren't optional extras you add once the technical skills are established. They're fundamental to how the technical skills get applied. A student who learns to sharpen perfectly but becomes frustrated when wood doesn't cooperate has missed something essential. The sharpening technique is explicit knowledge, teachable through demonstration. The composure when facing difficulty is tacit knowledge, absorbed through watching how a teacher responds to a challenge.

I try to model the attitudes I hope students develop. Patience with process, even when a piece is taking longer than expected. Respect for materials, treating wood as a partner rather than an obstacle. Curiosity about problems, seeing difficulties as puzzles rather than frustrations. Acceptance of mistakes, demonstrating how to recover rather than hiding failures. Willingness to experiment, trying approaches that might not work. These attitudes can't be taught directly through instruction. You can't lecture someone into patience or assign exercises in curiosity. They're absorbed through observation and participation. Students learn them by watching how you work, how you respond to challenges, how you talk about the craft. If I become frustrated with difficult wood, they learn that frustration is the appropriate response. If I remain calm, curious and adaptive, they learn that instead. The workshop is always teaching, whether I intend it or not.

I had a catch during a demonstration, left a visible gouge in what was supposed to be a finished surface. My first instinct was embarrassment, the urge to make excuses or start over with fresh wood. Instead, I stopped and said, "Right, that wasn't planned. Let's talk about options." We discussed whether it could be turned away, whether it could become a feature, whether the design could adapt. I showed them how I'd assess the damage, how I'd decide which approach to take. In the end, I turned it away by adjusting the design slightly. The piece was different from what I'd intended, but still good. Afterwards, club members said to me that the mistake taught them more than the rest of the demonstration. They saw that errors happen to everyone and that recovery is possible. That's worth more than a flawless performance that leaves them thinking mistakes are unacceptable.

There's also the challenge of teaching without imposing. Every teacher has preferences, biases, habitual approaches. I hold tools in particular ways, favour certain angles, prefer specific sequences of operations. These certainly aren't wrong, but they aren't the only ways. They developed from my body, my learning history, my aesthetic preferences. Another maker with different hands, different training, different goals might legitimately do things differently. Good teaching presents options rather than mandates. Here is how I approach this problem. Here are other approaches I've seen work well. Here are the trade-offs of each. Explore and find what works for you. This requires humility, admitting that your way isn't the only way or necessarily the best way for everyone. It also requires breadth, knowing enough about alternative approaches to present them fairly rather than dismissing them because they differ from your preference.

I've learnt more from teaching advanced students than beginners. Beginners need foundational skills: here is how you hold the tool, here is why this angle matters, here is the sequence of operations for a basic bowl. The questions are predictable because the learning needs are common. Advanced students ask harder questions. Why this way versus that way? How to solve unusual problems that don't fit standard approaches? When can rules be bent or broken? What distinguishes competent work from exceptional work?

These questions push my own thinking into new territory. Advanced students approach problems differently than I do, try methods I wouldn't have attempted, bring perspectives from other disciplines that illuminate aspects I hadn't seen. A student with art training sees proportion relationships I'd felt but not articulated. This reciprocal learning is one of teaching's great pleasures. You're not just giving. You're exchanging. The teaching relationship becomes a collaboration rather than a transmission.

There's also the pleasure of watching students go on to great things. I have students now who are running their own businesses, some on a small scale, one in particular is going great-guns and has started teaching, and has also been awarded a bursary from the Worshipful Company of Turners.

Passing knowledge on also means being honest about limitations. I don't know everything. Some questions I can't answer. Some techniques I haven't mastered. Some problems I haven't solved. Admitting this teaches students that perfection isn't required. Continuous learning is. Even experienced makers are still developing. Pretending to expertise you don't have does students no favours. It creates false expectations and models dishonesty. Better to say "I don't know, but here is how we might find out" than to bluff through uncertainty. Students learn from watching you navigate the edge of your knowledge as much as from watching you demonstrate established competence.

I've also learnt that different students need different approaches. Some learn by watching, absorbing visual information efficiently and translating observation into action. Others need to feel it in their hands, understanding through physical sensation rather than visual demonstration. Some need detailed explanation, wanting to understand why before attempting how. Others find too much talking confusing, preferring to try and adjust rather than analyse beforehand. Some learn best through structured progression, building skill systematically. Others learn best through projects, developing skills as needed to accomplish goals.

Now, I should be careful here. There's a popular idea called "learning styles" that suggests people are either visual learners or auditory learners or kinesthetic learners, and that teaching should be matched to each person's style. This idea is intuitive and appealing, but the research doesn't support it. A comprehensive review by Pashler and colleagues in 2008, published in Psychological Science in the Public Interest, examined the evidence and found no credible support for the claim that matching instruction to supposed learning styles improves outcomes[65]. Multiple studies since have confirmed this finding. The "meshing hypothesis," as researchers call it, simply doesn't hold up.

Here's what I've observed: while rigid learning style categories don't necessarily work, individual differences in how people approach learning are absolutely real. The mistake isn't in noticing that students differ. It's in assuming those differences are fixed traits that require permanently different instruction. What I see is more nuanced: the same student might benefit from visual demonstration for one technique and hands-on exploration for another. A student who needs detailed explanation when learning something unfamiliar might find too much talking distracting once they've grasped the basics. The differences are real but fluid, context-dependent, not permanent categories.

What works better than matching instruction to supposed styles is varying instruction for everyone. Cognitive scientists call this "multimodal" teaching. Show it, explain it, let them try it, discuss what happened. The combination serves all students better than any single approach. Richard Mayer's research on multimedia learning, summarised in his book "Multimedia Learning" (2009), demonstrates that people generally learn better from words and pictures together than from words alone, regardless of their supposed learning style[66].

What I've learnt is that student preferences are often not what they actually need. Someone who says they learn best by watching might actually need to try and fail. Someone who wants to dive in might benefit from slowing down to observe first. Good teaching isn't about matching instruction to preferences. It's about providing multiple pathways and helping students discover what actually works for them, which might be different from what they think works.

Good teaching adapts to each student rather than forcing everyone through identical methods. This requires attention to how each person is actually progressing, noticing what helps and what hinders, adjusting approach based on response rather than based on supposed categories. The same information delivered differently can transform confusion into clarity.

There's also timing. Teaching too much too fast overwhelms. Information piles up faster than it can be processed, creating confusion rather than capability. Teaching too little frustrates. Students ready for a challenge become bored with repetition, eager to advance but held back by overly cautious pacing. Finding the right pace, enough challenge to engage without so much that it discourages, takes experience and attention. Every class, and every student is different. What worked last time might not work this time. The same student might need different pacing on different days depending on energy, focus, or complexity of material. Flexibility serves teaching. Rigid adherence to predetermined plans ignores the reality that learning happens in real time and must be responded to in real time.

Documentation extends teaching beyond immediate presence. Writing, photographing, filming: these create knowledge that can reach people you'll never meet, in places you'll never visit, at times long after you're gone. This asynchronous teaching has different requirements than face-to-face instruction. It must be more complete because you can't fill gaps through conversation. It must be more explicit because you can't demonstrate what words fail to convey. It must be more anticipatory of questions you can't answer in real time, addressing confusions before they arise. But it extends your reach far beyond what personal instruction allows. A book or video can teach thousands while you sleep, continuing to share knowledge without requiring your presence.

The process of writing forces even deeper clarity than verbal teaching because you can't rely on gesture, on demonstration, on the feedback loop of watching understanding develop. Everything must be explicit on the page. But books also represent humility. By the time they publish, I've already learnt things that may change what I wrote. Understanding continues to develop even as the printed words remain fixed. Knowledge keeps evolving. No teaching is final. The best we can offer is our current understanding, honestly presented, with acknowledgement that future understanding will refine or revise it.

In a lesson, the student gains knowledge and capability. The teacher gains clarity and perspective. Each revolution of the lathe teaches the student something about wood, about tools, and themselves. Each question from a student teaches the teacher something about what they actually know, about how understanding can be communicated, about the gaps in their own expertise. The next revolution isn't just the wood spinning on the lathe. It's the turning over of knowledge from one person to another, changed in the transfer, alive in a way that hoarded knowledge never is.

27: The Long Apprenticeship

THERE ARE THINGS you can only learn through time. Not through reading or watching, not through intensive practice or careful study, but simply through years of doing. Experience accumulates in ways that can't be rushed. You can't compress decades into months no matter how diligently you work.

I turn differently now than I did when I started. I'm slower, more selective, and less driven by proving anything to anyone, including myself. I notice more because I've learnt what to look for. I make different choices about what to make and why because I understand what matters to me better than before.

The danger is assuming that experience alone brings wisdom. It doesn't. Experience brings information, a vast accumulation of observations about what works and what doesn't, how materials behave, what approaches succeed. Wisdom comes from reflecting on that information, from being willing to question what you've learnt, from staying open to new understanding even when it contradicts comfortable assumptions. Experience without reflection can just as easily calcify into habit as develop into wisdom[67]. You can do something for forty years and learn nothing after the first five if you stop paying attention.

I know turners with decades of experience who repeat the same approaches, the same forms, the same methods they learnt early on. They're experienced but not necessarily wise. They stopped learning years ago, settling into comfortable routines that no longer challenge them. Their experience accumulated but didn't deepen.

I'm thinking of a turner I've encountered at virtually every club. Thirty years of experience, competent and reliable work, but identical to what he was making a decade ago. He'd found what worked and stopped exploring. His experience had become a fortress rather than a foundation.

Wisdom requires continuous growth, not just continuous doing. It requires remaining curious even about things you think you understand, questioning your own practices, staying open to other, possibly better approaches.

What time teaches most clearly is perspective. In my early years of turning, every piece felt urgent. Success or failure seemed consequential, each project a test of my worth as a maker. Now I know each piece is one of thousands I'll make in a lifetime. Individual successes or failures matter less than the cumulative practice, the overall trajectory of development. This long view reduces anxiety and increases enjoyment. The work is important, but no single piece is critical. A failed piece is information, not a catastrophe. A successful vessel is satisfaction, not validation. This perspective only comes from having made enough pieces to see the pattern.

Time also teaches humility. The more you know, the more you recognise how much remains unknown. Early confidence often comes from ignorance. You think turning is simpler than it is because you haven't yet encountered its depths. Accumulated experience reveals complexity that was invisible initially, layers of nuance you couldn't perceive when you were focused on basics. Wisdom is knowing how much you don't know[68]. It's understanding that mastery is limitless, something you approach forever without ever fully reaching.

There's also patience that comes with time. Early on, I wanted immediate results. Impatience drove me to rush, to skip steps, to force progress faster than it wanted to come. Now I know that good work takes time and can't be hurried without cost. This patience isn't resignation or passivity. It's the acceptance of reality. Wood behaves on its own timeline, drying at its own pace, moving as it adjusts to new conditions. Skills develop through their own stages, with plateaus that precede breakthroughs. Fighting these realities wastes energy and creates frustration. Working with them produces better results with less struggle.

Experience teaches you to recognise patterns. Wood species behave predictably once you've worked with them enough times. Certain mistakes recur across different projects and different makers. Specific approaches work reliably in specific situations. This pattern recognition develops only through accumulation of many examples. You can't shortcut it. You have to see enough instances to recognise what they have in common, to distinguish signal from noise, to know which variations matter and which are incidental.

But pattern recognition can also become limitation if you let it. If you always approach problems the same way because that way has worked before, you stop seeing new possibilities. You become efficient but not innovative. Wisdom means using patterns as starting points rather than destinations. Experience suggests likely approaches, provides hypotheses worth testing first. But each situation still deserves fresh attention. Each piece of wood is unique. Each project has its own requirements. Experienced makers balance what they know with openness to what they might learn.

I've also learnt through time that mistakes are information, not judgement. When something goes wrong, it's showing you something: a gap in understanding, a limitation in technique, a property of the material you hadn't fully appreciated. Early on, mistakes felt like personal failings, evidence of inadequacy, reasons for shame. Now they feel like education. The piece that catches teaches more than the piece that goes smoothly. The form that fails reveals something about proportion that success might have hidden. This shift from judgement to curiosity makes learning from experience possible. As long as mistakes feel like failure, you avoid them or hide them. When they feel like information, you examine them and extract their lessons.

Time teaches specificity too. Vague terms like "good" or "balanced" become inadequate as your perception refines. You develop vocabulary for describing what you see and feel with precision. This curve is too quick, meaning it accelerates too rapidly. This proportion is too heavy, meaning the base overwhelms the form. This transition is too abrupt, meaning the eye can't follow it comfortably. Precise language enables precise thinking, which enables precise work. The ability to articulate exactly what's wrong with something is the first step toward fixing it.

There's also the accumulation of near-misses and saves. Experienced makers have recovered from countless problems. They've saved pieces that seemed ruined, found solutions to situations that appeared hopeless, turned accidents into features. This history builds confidence. You know you can often save a piece because you've done it before. You know that apparent disaster is frequently recoverable because you've recovered before.

This confidence allows risk-taking that inexperience can't afford. You can push boundaries knowing that going too far is usually survivable.

What time gives most clearly is proportion about your own development. You can see your growth over years rather than days. The anxiety about today's failures diminishes when you can see last year's failures and this year's competence. You trust growth because you've seen it happen, because you've lived through enough cycles of struggle and breakthrough to know the pattern. This long-term perspective supports patience with current struggles.

Whatever you're wrestling with now, you'll probably understand better in a year. That knowledge comes from having experienced exactly that pattern repeatedly.

Experience also teaches the value of fundamentals. I've spent time exploring advanced techniques, unusual methods, and complex projects that pushed boundaries. These explorations were valuable, teaching me about limits and possibilities. But I keep returning to basics: good tool control, clean cuts, proper sharpening, careful finishing. Advanced work is built on fundamentals, and fundamentals never stop mattering no matter how experienced you become. The master returns to basics not because they've forgotten them but because they understand their importance more deeply than ever.

There's also acceptance that comes with time. Some limitations are permanent. I'll never have certain talents that come naturally to others. Some skills will always be harder for me, requiring extra effort where others work easily. Early on, this felt like failure, like evidence that I wasn't meant for this work. Now it feels like reality, simply the shape of who I am. I work with my capabilities rather than fighting them, developing strengths rather than agonising over weaknesses. I am left-handed, after all, and lathes are made for right-handed people, so learning to turn has always been a bit of a challenge, perhaps more so than if I had been right-handed. This acceptance is liberating rather than limiting. Energy spent wishing you were different is energy unavailable for actual improvement.

Time has also taught me about cycles. Periods of productivity alternate with periods of consolidation. Times of inspiration when ideas flow faster than you can execute them alternate with times of simply showing up and working through the day's tasks. Creative surges give way to technical refinement. These cycles are natural, part of how creative work unfolds over years[69]. Fighting them is exhausting and futile. Accepting them makes the work sustainable over decades rather than burning out in years. The dry periods pass. The inspiration returns. Trusting this requires having lived through enough cycles to know the pattern holds.

I can feel the difference now between phases. A productive phase has energy, momentum, a sense of possibility. Ideas generate more ideas. One finished piece suggests three more. I work longer hours without noticing, carried by enthusiasm. A consolidation phase feels different: quieter, steadier, more about maintenance than creation. I'm sharpening tools, organising the workshop, making pieces I've made before rather than exploring new territory. Early in my turning life, I thought the consolidation phases were problems, signs that something was wrong, that I'd lost whatever creative spark I once had (think writer's block here. It is very similar). Now I recognise them as necessary. The productive phases draw down reserves that the consolidation phases replenish. You can't stay in a creative surge forever. The quieter periods are recovery, preparation for the next surge.

I've learnt too that teaching your younger self is futile. I can't make my early self understand what I know now. That self needed to go through what they went through to arrive here. The struggles I would spare them are precisely what created the understanding I now have. Similarly, I can't fully understand what my future self will know. I'm always leaning toward understanding I don't yet possess. This humility about the limits of current knowledge is itself a form of wisdom that only time teaches.

Looking at work from years ago produces a curious double vision. I see both how far I've come and how much I still didn't understand even when I thought I knew a lot. A piece I was proud of at the time now reveals limitations I was blind to then. This perspective is simultaneously encouraging (look how much progress happened) and humbling (there's still so much to learn). Both feelings are appropriate. Both are valuable. They remind me that current understanding is also incomplete, that future perspective will reveal blindnesses I can't currently see.

Experience teaches patience in ways that theory can't. You know from direct evidence that skills improve with practice, that understanding deepens over time, that problems which seem insurmountable now will become manageable with continued work. This isn't belief or hope but knowledge based on having lived through exactly that process repeatedly. This experiential knowledge sustains you through difficult periods because you've been through difficulty before and emerged more capable. You trust the process because you've seen it work.

I think about the turners I admired early in my development. They seemed to know everything, to work effortlessly, to never make mistakes. Now, decades later and knowing some of them personally, I understand they struggled just as I did. They just had more experience managing struggle. They knew that most problems are solvable, that persistence produces results, that apparent setbacks often lead to unexpected progress. That knowledge came from experience, from decades of working through challenges and seeing what emerged. What looked like effortlessness was actually deep familiarity with difficulty.

So experience is an ongoing teacher, always offering new lessons if you remain attentive. The question isn't whether you have enough experience but whether you're learning from the experience you have. Are you noticing patterns? Are you questioning assumptions? Are you willing to revise understanding based on new evidence? Are you staying curious about things you think you already know? This active engagement with experience is what transforms mere duration into genuine wisdom. Ten years of learning produces something very different from one year repeated ten times.

The wisdom of experience ultimately includes knowing that experience itself isn't enough. Accumulated years don't automatically produce wisdom. Time teaches only those willing to be taught. Wisdom requires reflection on experience, willingness to question assumptions, openness to new information, humility about limitations. Experience provides raw material. Wisdom is what you build from that material through ongoing attention and thought. The workshop keeps teaching. The question is whether you keep learning.

28: Making as Meditation

THERE'S A QUALITY of attention in making that resembles meditation. Complete presence, full engagement with the moment, quieting of the constant mental chatter[70]. The lathe demands this. You can't turn well while thinking about something else. You have to be here, now, paying attention to what's actually happening rather than what happened yesterday or might happen tomorrow.

This is one of the great gifts of craftwork. It pulls you out of worry about the past or the future and anchors you in the present. The wood spinning, the tool in your hands, the sound of the cut, the feel of shavings brushing past: these are immediate, tangible, real. Everything else fades. For that time at the lathe, you're fully present in a way that modern life rarely allows or demands.

I don't make claims about turning being spiritual or transformative in any grand sense. But I do know that time at the lathe provides relief from the constant mental noise that characterises modern life. It creates space for calm, for focus, for being rather than endlessly doing and planning and worrying. And in that space, something restores itself. Not dramatically, but genuinely. You emerge from a good session feeling different than you went in.

The parallels with formal meditation are notable[71]. Both involve focusing attention on immediate experience rather than abstract thought. Both require letting thoughts pass without attachment, noticing them and returning to presence rather than following them down rabbit holes. Both develop capacity for sustained concentration that transfers to other areas of life. The difference is that turning produces objects while meditation produces only a mental state. But the attention skills are remarkably similar, and I suspect practitioners of either would recognise the other's experience.

I notice this most when I'm anxious or overwhelmed. Turning pulls me out of mental spiralling into physical presence. I can't worry effectively about future problems while paying attention to current cuts. The work demands too much attention to allow divided focus. This forced presence is therapeutic in a way that trying not to worry never achieves. The mind can't be empty, but it can be fully occupied with something real and immediate. That occupation provides relief that direct attempts at calm can't.

My main problem when I get anxious or overwhelmed is actually starting the lathe and making something. I know the act of turning will help me, but getting started is the difficult bit.

There's also the question of breath. In meditation, breath awareness anchors attention to the present moment. In turning, the same principle applies. When cutting goes well, breath is easy and regular, flowing naturally without conscious direction. When tension builds, whether from difficult wood or approaching a delicate section, breath becomes shallow or held entirely. Noticing breath provides instant feedback about mental and physical state. Returning attention to breath, consciously breathing through challenging moments, restores the calm that enables good work. The breath is always available as anchor, in meditation and at the lathe alike.

The repetitive nature of some turning operations particularly resembles formal meditation practice. Sanding through grits, applying multiple coats of finish, turning production pieces where the same form repeats: these tasks are meditative through their very repetition. The mind settles into rhythm. Thoughts still arise, as they always do, but they don't stick. They pass through without disrupting the work or demanding engagement. You're working but also resting. The hands are busy while the mind is quiet. This combination produces a particular kind of restoration that neither pure rest nor pure mental engagement can match.

This meditative quality is why time in the workshop often feels restorative even though it's physically demanding. The work tires the body while resting the mind from its usual churning. This combination produces a different kind of exhaustion than mental work, satisfying rather than depleting. You finish tired but refreshed, a paradox that makes perfect sense once you've experienced it. The exhaustion is clean, earned through actual making rather than through the circular futility of worry.

But making as meditation requires intention. You can't turn while mentally elsewhere, worrying about tomorrow's meeting, planning next week's projects, ruminating on yesterday's frustrations. This divided attention prevents the meditative quality and usually produces inferior work besides. Presence must be cultivated deliberately. Returning attention to the work when it wanders is the practice, just as meditation involves returning attention to breath when thoughts arise. The wandering isn't failure.

The quality of this meditative state varies. Some days, presence comes easily and sustains naturally through hours of work. Other days, attention is fractured and requires constant bringing back, thought after thought pulling me away and needing gentle redirection. Both are part of practice. The goal isn't perfect meditation but an ongoing attempt at presence. Even an imperfect presence is valuable, far better than no attempt at all. The practice is in the returning, not in never wandering.

Making as meditation also involves acceptance. The wood is what it is, with its particular grain and figure and quirks.

Your skill level is what it is, developed to exactly where it has developed so far. The piece will be what it will be, emerging from the collaboration between your intention and reality's constraints. This acceptance of reality as it is, rather than as you wish it were, is fundamental to both meditation and making[72]. Fighting reality creates suffering. Accepting it creates space for actually working with what exists.

I've found that this acceptance doesn't mean passivity or lowered standards. You still work skilfully, make good choices, and pursue excellence. But you release attachment to specific outcomes. You do your best and accept results without demanding they match some predetermined ideal. This paradox, caring deeply while remaining unattached to particular outcomes, is at the heart of both meditation and craftsmanship. It isn't indifference but a different kind of caring, one that doesn't create additional suffering when reality differs from hope.

When conditions align, when skills match challenge, when attention is focused, and external distractions are minimal, time disappears. Hours feel like minutes. The work absorbs you completely. This flow state is one of life's great pleasures, and turning provides unusual access to it because it demands full attention while offering clear and immediate feedback. You know instantly whether a cut worked. There's no ambiguity, no waiting for results, no wondering if you did it right. The wood tells you immediately. This tight feedback loop supports flow in ways that more abstract work can't match.

I remember one session in particular. I was turning a set of pieces for a big event near Southampton. I started mid-morning. The first bowl took shape, then the second. By the time I was refining the fifth or sixth piece, I noticed the light had changed. I looked at my watch: four hours had passed. It felt like forty minutes. I hadn't thought about lunch, hadn't noticed my phone, hadn't been aware of anything except the wood and the tool and the emerging forms. When I finally stopped, I had a handful of completed pieces and a few more roughed out. I was physically exhausted but mentally clearer than I'd been in weeks. That's what flow feels like: time compression, total absorption, and emergence into a kind of clarity.

I notice that workshop sessions where I achieve flow are dramatically more productive than sessions where I'm merely working. Not because I'm working faster but because I'm working more efficiently. No wasted motion. No false starts. No second-guessing. The work simply flows from intention through hands into wood without friction or hesitation. That efficiency comes from total presence, from attention that's complete but not effortful. You're not trying hard. You're just fully there.

The meditative quality also provides perspective on other life challenges. Problems that seem overwhelming when you're thinking about them often shrink to manageable size when you're working. The hands are busy, the mind is occupied with immediate reality, and somehow solutions appear that conscious analysis couldn't find. This isn't magic. It's allowing unconscious processing to work while my conscious mind is otherwise engaged, giving the deeper mind space to work on problems without the interference of anxious attention.

I've solved more problems while turning than while sitting and thinking about those problems. Something about the rhythm of work, the engagement with material, and the necessity of being present allows a different kind of thinking. Not analytical thinking but intuitive understanding that arrives whole rather than being constructed piece by piece.

Quite often, if I am struggling with a business decision, going round in circles for days, analysing options, making lists, lying awake at night, I give up thinking about it and go to the workshop. The simple, repetitive cuts require attention but not much thought. At some point, the answer to my struggle usually appears. Not as a conclusion reached through argument, but as clarity that was suddenly just there. I know what to do. I can't explain why, but the knowing is solid. I follow it, and most of the time, it's right.

This is valuable beyond workshop walls. Learning to access this intuitive knowing through meditative making transfers to other domains where pure analysis fails or exhausts itself.

There's also the meditative quality of accepting impermanence. The piece you're working on now won't last forever. Neither will you. Neither will the tradition itself eventually. This impermanence could be depressing but can instead be liberating. Since nothing lasts, the value lies in the doing rather than in the result alone. The meditation happens in the work itself, not just in possessing the finished piece. This perspective changes everything about why and how you make. The making becomes its own purpose, not just means to an end.

So while I don't make spiritual claims about turning, I recognise that the attention it requires, the presence it demands, the calm it produces, the flow it enables: these are the same qualities meditation cultivates. Whether you frame it as meditation or simply as focused work, the experience is similar. And in a world of constant distraction, any practice that develops sustained attention is valuable beyond its immediate products.

29: Still Learning

THE MOST ACCOMPLISHED turners I know are the ones who still ask questions. Not rhetorical questions designed to show how much they understand, but genuine ones. How did you get that surface? What would happen if I tried it this way? Why does this wood behave differently from that one? Their curiosity is alive in a way that has nothing to do with how many years they've been at the lathe.

I try to stay one of those people. Some days I manage it better than others.

Learning doesn't arrive automatically just because you keep showing up. You can turn for decades and stop learning after the first few years, settling into comfortable patterns that no longer challenge you. Continued learning requires intention. It requires putting yourself in situations where you don't already know the answer.

The most reliable source of learning, for me, has been students. This sounds backwards. I'm supposed to be teaching them. But their questions sometimes expose gaps in my understanding that I didn't know existed. When a student struggles with something I find easy, I'm forced to break it down into components I stopped thinking about ages ago. When they ask why we do something a particular way, I sometimes realise I don't actually know. I've just always done it that way.

This is why teaching deepens understanding rather than just distributing it[73]. You discover what you actually know versus what you only thought you knew.

Other crafts offer another rich source of learning. Woodturning doesn't exist in isolation. The principles that govern good form are universal. How potters think about curves, how metalworkers approach surface finish, how furniture makers consider grain orientation: all of these have lessons that transfer directly to the lathe if you're paying attention.

The most useful insight I've borrowed came from cooking, of all places. A chef I spotted on social media explained mise en place[74]: having everything prepared and in place before you start. Ingredients measured, tools ready, sequence planned. This prevents the scrambling that happens when you discover mid-process that something isn't where you need it.

If you have everything prepared before you start a session with tools sharpened, blanks selected, finishing supplies accessible etc, then the work flows smoothly because you're not stopping to sharpen shortly after starting or hunting for abrasives. That simple idea transformed my workflow, and it came from a kitchen, not a workshop.

Reading widely contributes too. Not just turning books (I have a few project-based ones rather than technique-based ones), though those matter, but design theory that articulates why certain forms satisfy the eye. Material science that explains how wood behaves and why. Philosophy of craft that examines what making means beyond the objects produced. History that shows how traditions developed and what earlier makers discovered through trial and error, we can now simply inherit.

Theory and practice need each other. You can't learn turning just from books any more than you can learn swimming from reading about it. But practice without theory is just repetition. The knowledge has to move from page to hands, from concept to capability, through actual doing. Both matter. Neither is sufficient alone.

Then there's unlearning, which might be harder than learning in the first place.

Some of what I learnt early turned out to be wrong. Not completely wrong, but inefficient, or only right in specific circumstances I'd generalised too broadly. Correcting these ingrained habits under professional guidance required admitting that what I thought I knew was incomplete. That was uncomfortable as it felt like I was moving backwards.

Unlearning requires holding knowledge lightly. Treating what you know as provisional[75], always subject to revision when a better understanding emerges. This is harder than it sounds. We become attached to our expertise. Admitting that something we've learnt (or taught ourselves) and built our identity around might be wrong or incomplete takes a kind of courage that has nothing to do with skill level.

There's also the question of what to learn. You can't learn everything. Time is finite, attention is limited, and choices have to be made.

I've recently chosen to go deep on form and proportion. Understanding why certain shapes satisfy the eye and others don't. This means studying design principles, analysing work I admire, and experimenting endlessly with curves and transitions. In the past, I've gone deep on finishing, particularly approaches using my own manufactured products. These choices reflect what I care about: pieces that feel right visually and honour the material through appropriate surface treatment.

Conversely, I've deliberately stayed shallow on ornamental techniques. I can do texturing, pyrography, and advanced colouring with dyes, airbrushes, paints and sprays. But I haven't invested in fully mastering these areas because they don't serve the work I want to make. When students ask about ornamental turning, I can take them to a point past the basics then send them off toward more experienced resources. I've learnt enough to satisfy my needs for most of my work. This is simply a strategic choice about where to invest limited time. If I need to learn more about something, I will invest the time when I need to.

Going deep somewhere serves better than going shallow everywhere[76]. You become more capable by developing genuine expertise in chosen areas than by accumulating superficial familiarity across everything.

Learning also requires vulnerability. Admitting you don't know something, asking questions that might seem basic to others. All of this means setting aside ego.

Pride prevents learning by making ignorance shameful[77]. If you can't admit what you don't know, you can't address it. Humility enables learning by making ignorance acceptable: just another starting point rather than a character flaw. The willingness to be a beginner again and again, even in areas where you have experience, keeps learning possible throughout a lifetime.

I remember the first time I attended an advanced workshop after I'd been teaching for a while. Part of me felt I should already know everything being covered. What would the other people there think if they saw me struggling with techniques, asking basic questions?

That insecurity nearly kept me from going. I'm glad it didn't. I learnt more in that workshop than in the previous six months of working alone. And no one thought less of me for being there as a student. If anything, they respected that I was still willing to learn.

The trick is finding situations that stretch you. Comfortable repetition of what you already know doesn't produce learning. It produces efficiency, which has value, but it's not the same thing. Learning happens at the edge of your current capability, where success isn't guaranteed[78], where you have to figure things out rather than execute what you already understand.

This means deliberately seeking challenges. Taking on projects slightly beyond your current skill. Trying techniques you haven't mastered. Working with unfamiliar materials that don't behave the way you expect. Each of these creates the conditions where learning becomes possible.

It also means paying attention when things go wrong. Failures teach more than successes if you examine them carefully. Success confirms what you already knew. Failure reveals what you don't yet understand. The piece that catches, the form that doesn't work, the finish that goes wrong: these are all information about gaps in your knowledge. Treating them as education rather than an annoyance is how learning continues regardless of experience level.

I still make mistakes. Still ruin the occasional piece, still encounter problems I don't immediately know how to solve. The difference between now and when I started isn't that these things stopped happening. It's that they no longer feel catastrophic. They're just part of the process, the price of continuing to push rather than settling into safe repetition.

There's a particular pleasure in learning something new after years of practice. It's different from the overwhelming novelty of being a complete beginner, when everything is new and nothing is solid. It's more like finding a new room in a house you thought you knew completely. Surprise mixed with recognition. The satisfaction of the craft revealing another layer of depth you hadn't suspected was there.

That pleasure is what makes continued learning feel like privilege rather than obligation. The craft is inexhaustible. There's always more to discover if you stay curious enough to look. The only limit is whether you're willing to keep asking questions, keep admitting what you don't know, keep putting yourself in situations where learning becomes possible.

Still learning, then, isn't a confession of inadequacy. It's a description of how to stay engaged with work across decades. It's a practice, something you do deliberately, not something that happens automatically. It requires intention, humility, and the willingness to be uncomfortable.

The lathe keeps teaching. The wood keeps offering lessons. Other makers keep demonstrating possibilities you hadn't considered. Are you still paying attention?

I hope I always am.

30: The Circle Continues

EVERY PIECE YOU finish becomes part of a lineage. The techniques you use were developed by turners before you, refined through generations, passed along through teaching and example and the quiet evidence of completed work[79]. The forms you make will influence turners who come after, whether through direct instruction or simply through existing in the world as examples of what's possible. You're part of a continuum, a tradition that extends far beyond your individual practice in both directions.

I think about this when teaching. The students I work with may go on to teach others, formally in workshops or informally through the work they make and share. The approaches they learn from me will spread, evolve, and adapt to new circumstances and new makers. What I pass on doesn't end with them. It continues, changing as it moves forward through time, but maintaining some connection to its origins. This continuation is how craft knowledge survives across generations, how understanding developed decades ago reaches makers not yet born.

This perspective helps with the temporary nature of making. The pieces themselves may not last forever. Wood degrades over decades or centuries. Accidents happen, objects break, fires destroy. Tastes change and what was treasured may eventually become unwanted. But the knowledge, the attention to craft, the care in making: these things persist in ways that physical objects can't. They live in everyone who takes the time to work well, to pay attention, and to respect materials and processes. The tradition is carried not primarily in objects but in practices[80].

So when I turn, I'm not just making objects. I'm participating in something larger, a conversation across time between people who care about making things well. The lathe continues spinning long after any individual maker retires. The wood continues becoming, transformed from raw material to finished piece by hands that change while the process endures. The craft continues teaching anyone willing to learn. That continuity is perhaps the most meaningful aspect of all this work. Not the individual pieces, however beautiful. Not the personal satisfaction, however real. But the participation in something that transcends an individual's lifetime.

The understanding I have gained will be passed on through students who will carry it forward, through my writing that will outlast conversations, and through the pieces I've made that may influence other makers. The tradition I joined will continue through others who never knew me but who may benefit from what was passed along. My participation in the ongoing tradition connects me to something that endures beyond any individual.

This is why teaching matters so much. It's how an individual's knowledge becomes part of the collective knowledge. It's how temporary lives participate in permanent tradition. What you learn doesn't die with you if you pass it on. It continues, adapted and refined by others, changed by each transmission, but recognisable as part of the lineage. Teaching isn't just sharing information. It's ensuring the survival of understanding across time.

There's humility in this perspective. You're not the origin of the tradition, nor its culmination, nor its most important practitioner. You're a link in a circle stretching back centuries and forward into an unknowable future. That circle is stronger than any individual point on it, but it depends on each point being sound. Your part is small in the scale of the whole tradition, but necessary for the circle to remain unbroken. This perspective makes work feel both significant and appropriately modest, both meaningful and not too self-important.

I met a young turner at a demonstration a few years ago. He was perhaps thirteen or fourteen. I can't remember now. He'd been turning for a couple of years, largely self-taught from YouTube videos, working on a cheap lathe in his parents' garage. His technique was rough, but his enthusiasm was extraordinary. He asked questions for ages after my demonstration, hungry for understanding, and I gave as much information as I could in what time was available.

A few months later, he sent me a photograph of a piece he'd made. The proportions were good. The surface was clean. But what struck me was the note that came with it: he'd helped a friend try turning, and they loved it. Some knowledge had already moved one step further.

That moment crystallised something for me. In that simple act of giving a friend a go on his lathe, the tradition continued a little. Not through grand gestures or formal teaching, but through the quiet transfer of understanding from one person to another. A little of what I knew had become his own, and now his friend was beginning to show interest. There is the circle expanding outward, each person both receiving and giving, learning and teaching.

Legacy is not really monuments or museums, but moments. A tip shared between friends. A technique demonstrated at a club meeting. A video watched by someone you'll never meet. A book read by someone not yet born when you wrote it. These small transmissions, multiplied across countless interactions, are how traditions survive. They're how understanding developed by anonymous makers centuries ago reaches you today, filtered through thousands of hands but still recognisable, still useful and still very much alive.

The lineage isn't just technical. It's also philosophical. The patience required for good work, the respect for material that shapes how you approach it, the attention to detail that distinguishes craft from mere production, the pursuit of quality for its own sake rather than for external reward: these attitudes are as important as the techniques. They create the culture of craft that sustains the technical knowledge. Both must be passed forward together. Technique without attitude produces competent emptiness. Attitude without technique produces well-meaning failure.

Every tradition risks dying. If no one continues it, it stops. Skills that took centuries to develop can be lost in a single generation if no one bothers to learn them. This is why encouraging new makers matters so much. They are the continuity. Their participation ensures that what we know isn't lost when our generation passes. Supporting them isn't just helping individuals develop. It's maintaining tradition, ensuring the circle continues, keeping alive knowledge that would otherwise disappear.

There's also the question of evolution. Traditions that don't evolve die even if people continue practising them, becoming irrelevant relics rather than living practices. So continuity requires both preservation and innovation. Respecting what came before while finding what comes next by honouring traditional forms while exploring new possibilities. This tension between tradition and innovation is creative rather than problematic. It's how traditions stay alive through changing circumstances, adapting to new materials, tools, and contexts while maintaining their essential character.

The circle also includes the wood itself. Trees that grew decades or centuries ago, responding to seasons and weather, adding rings year by year, developing character through their particular circumstances. Cut down, dried, shaped into pieces that will be used for years or decades.

Then eventually returning to the earth, decomposing, nourishing new growth that might someday become material for future makers. Turning is one stage in this transformation cycle that extends far beyond human timescales. Your work participates in natural processes larger than any individual life.

I have a piece of Irish bog oak in the workshop. It is roughly as old as some of the pyramids and one of the phases of Stonehenge. There's also a bowl at home made from an oak that stood for three hundred years before a storm brought it down. The tree was growing when Newton was working on his theories, and I have some petrified wood that is some 350 million years old. We are just a brief moment in those materials' long journeys. Using a lathe to make something from timber is a temporary form that the wood passes through. I wouldn't fancy turning the petrified wood, though, as it has turned to stone now!

There's also the community of current makers, the horizontal dimension of the circle alongside its vertical extension through time. We're all part of the same moment in the tradition's history. Our conversations, our shared challenges, our different approaches to similar problems: these constitute the tradition's current expression. We're writing this chapter together even though we may never meet, scattered across geography but connected by common practice.

I feel a connection to turners I'll never know. Ancestors in the tradition who faced similar challenges with cruder tools. Contemporaries around the world are solving similar problems in different ways, with different woods, in different contexts. Future makers who will face the same fundamental questions about form, material, and meaning that have always defined the craft. We're all part of the same conversation across time and space, contributors to understanding that no individual could develop alone.

The circle continues because making satisfies something fundamental in human nature[81]. The desire to shape material, to create useful beauty, to work with hands and mind together, to leave evidence of care in a physical form: these seem universal across cultures and time. As long as humans exist, someone will be making something. Someone will be turning wood on a lathe or whatever future technology provides. That continuity is reassuring. The tradition is larger than any threat to it, sustained by human nature itself.

So when I finish a piece, clean the workshop, and put away tools, I'm not ending something. I'm pausing. The work will continue tomorrow, next week, next year, and next generation. My work will continue through others even after I can't continue it myself, carried forward by everyone I taught and everyone they teach and everyone influenced by work I made. The circle has no end because it's sustained by everyone who participates in it.

I think of that young turner sometimes, and wonder what he's making now, whether he's still introducing his friends. I think of all the students who've passed through the school, each carrying forward some fragment of what we explored together in the workshop.

I think of everyone who's watched a video online by someone on the other side of the world, read an article in a magazine or a fifteen-year-old blog post, picked up a tip that helped them make something better for someone, shared a photo, or asked for advice on social media... All of these connections, visible and invisible, form the web that holds the tradition together.

That participation, adding your efforts to centuries of efforts, joining hands across time with everyone who has cared about making well, is perhaps the deepest satisfaction of craft. Deeper than the pleasure of a well-turned piece, deeper than the satisfaction of a problem solved or a skill mastered. You're part of something that was here before you and will continue after you. You contributed to its continuation. You helped ensure it survives.

That isn't small. That's enough. That's everything.

Demonstrating via the internet helps reach turners all over the world. My old workshop, 2022.

Part Six

The End Stuff

Epilogue

BOOKS NEED ENDINGS. This is mine.

Everything in these pages has come from trying things and paying attention to what happened. I've pushed boundaries, experimented with forms I wasn't sure would work, taken on projects that stretched me further than felt comfortable. Some failed, but thankfully most succeeded. All of them taught me something, but the failures taught me more than the successes ever did. When something works, you understand why. When something fails, you know where to improve, where to practice, how to get better.

This is how proficiency develops. Not in sudden leaps, but through accumulation. Each piece builds on the last. Each problem solved becomes a tool for solving the next. The progression is rarely visible day to day, but look back over a year, and the distance covered is remarkable. Skills that once demanded all your concentration become automatic, freeing your attention for subtler challenges. What felt impossible becomes achievable, then comfortable, then the foundation for attempting something harder still.

I've built a life and businesses around a craft I stumbled into by accident one spring day in 2014. I've made things I'm proud of, and taught students who've gone on to wonderful things in their turning careers. None of it came from playing safe or waiting until I felt ready.

If you take one thing from this book, let it be this: *Start.* Then keep going. Don't wait until you know enough, have the right tools, find the perfect wood, or feel ready. You won't. The learning happens in the *doing,* not in the preparation for doing. And the real growth happens when you attempt something just beyond your current ability.

After twelve years at the lathe, my own growth has

shifted. The technical challenges that once consumed me are now solved. What stretches me now is finding better ways to share what I've learnt, to communicate clearly what my hands understand intuitively. Writing this book was part of that. Teaching is part of it most days of the week. The craft keeps asking more of me, just in different ways than it used to.

That's the work. It evolves, but it doesn't end. You do it, you learn, you push a bit further, you do it again.

Thank you for reading. See you at the lathe.

Dedication

NO CRAFT, NO book, and no person stands alone. Every insight in these pages owes something to others: friends, teachers, students, and makers who have shaped the way I see and the way I work. Some knowingly. Others probably without realising they were teaching me anything at all.

To Les Thorne, whose blunt but thoughtful criticism has sharpened my thinking since 2016 and whose friendship and unofficial mentorship have meant more than I've probably ever said properly. To the many makers who have taught me through their work, their patience, or simply by letting me watch. Many of their lessons live in these pages, even if their names aren't written here.

To the students who have shared time with me at The Woodturning School: thank you for your curiosity, your good humour, and for reminding me that teaching has never been a one-way exchange.

To everyone who has watched a video, left a comment, read an article, or joined my Woodturning360 club: thank you for proving that woodturning connects people across oceans and generations. Your encouragement has kept this work turning, sometimes when I needed it most.

To my family, for endlessly pretending to understand the long hours, the dust, and the quiet obsession that comes with this life. And for not complaining too much about the shavings I track through the house.

To Xander and Clara, my children who continually inspire me through their resilience, determination, and the sheer strength to head wherever they want to go, with the energy and ambition their youth affords them.

About the Author

MARTIN SABAN-SMITH IS a professional woodturner, teacher, and author based in Hampshire, UK. He is a member of the Register of Professional Turners and runs The Woodturning School, where students learn in a workshop built for proper teaching with enough space to make mistakes without elbowing the person next to you.

He came to woodturning in 2014 after two decades as a professional photographer and designer, a background that shaped his approach from the start. He thinks about form and proportion instinctively, designs before he turns, and believes that how a piece looks matters just as much as how it was made. His first book, *Woodturning: Form and Formula,* explores the role of the Golden Ratio and Rule of Thirds in turning, treating them as gentle guides rather than rigid rules.

Martin's YouTube channel (@msabansmith) has grown to have a loyal following of makers who appreciate both the practical techniques and the occasional honest disaster.

Having started a company making wood finishes called Hampshire Sheen in 2015 and exporting the products to major European and North American marketplaces, he closed it down in 2025. Sadly, legislative changes in the EU and governmental changes in the UK and US made business far too difficult for a one-man-band to continue.

In 2020, he founded Woodturning360, an online club that brings together turners from across 11 countries who share a love of learning and a willingness to help each other improve.

He has demonstrated at events and clubs across the whole of the UK and internationally (USA, Ireland, Sweden, Denmark and Netherlands), as well as a lot of online streaming to overseas clubs and for free through social media, and served

as guest editor for Woodturning Magazine.
His teaching philosophy is straightforward: process matters more than perfection, community matters more than competition, and the best time to start is whenever you're ready.
When not turning, Martin can usually be found planning his next workshop course, sketching designs he may or may not get around to making, or down by the water with a fishing rod, enjoying the one hobby that might actually require more patience than woodturning.

Learn more at:
* www.msabansmith.com
* www.thewoodturning.school
* www.woodturning360.com
* www.youtube.com/@msabansmith

The craft survives because people talk about it, show it, and pass it on. Every demonstration is a small act of keeping the circle turning.

These notes have been collated from researching various things when writing the book and backup whether or not what I was thinking about had any evidence to back it up.

---

[1] **Zen Mind, Beginner's Mind.**
When we start learning, we're curious and open; shoshin eliminates biases that impede creativity.
Shunryu Suzuki / Buddhism.
http://www.lionsroar.com/buddhism/beginners-mind/

[2] **Muscle Memory and the Brain.**
Deliberate practice strengthens neural connections; basal ganglia and cerebellum coordinate movement learning.
Journal of Advanced Medical & Dental Sciences Research.
https://jamdsr.com/uploadfiles/66vol7issue9pp273-27920230623061409.pdf

[3] **Appearance Wood Products and Psychological Well-Being.**
Wood emotionally uplifting, associated with comfort and health.
Rice, Kozak, Meitner & Cohen.
www.researchgate.net/publication/241779924_Appearance_wood_products_and_psychological_well-being

[4] **Wood Movement and Moisture Content.**
Technical understanding of how wood responds to environment.
https://www.woodmagazine.com/wood-movement

[5] **Touch to Learn: Haptic Technology Review.**
Haptic feedback improves fine motor control; tactile learning engages multiple brain regions.
Hatira et al.
https://advanced.onlinelibrary.wiley.com/doi/10.1002/aisy.202300731

[6] **Chatoyance.**
Coined from the French *œil de chat*, meaning cat's eye, the chatoyant effect is typically characterised by one or more well-defined bands of reflected light.
https://en.wikipedia.org/wiki/Chatoyancy

[7] **Biophilia Hypothesis.**
Humans have innate tendency to seek connections with nature; explains satisfaction from working with wood.
Wikipedia / E.O. Wilson.
https://en.wikipedia.org/wiki/Biophilia_hypothesis

[8] **Deliberate Practice Theory.**
Expertise development through focused practice; importance of intentional repetition.
K. Anders Ericksson.
https://psycnet.apa.org/record/1993-40718-001

[9] **Spindle Roughing Gouge on a Bowl.**

This tool is not designed for use on a bowl owing to it's weak tang.

[10] **Tacit Knowledge in Psychology.**
Tacit knowledge implicit; analysis of skilful feat always incomplete.
ScienceDirect / Polanyi
https://www.sciencedirect.com/topics/psychology/tacit-knowledge

[11] **Embodied Cognition.**
Body plays significant role in cognitive abilities; knowledge rooted in physical experience.
Stanford Encyclopedia of Philosophy.
https://plato.stanford.edu/entries/embodied-cognition/

[12] **Neurobiological Changes from Mindfulness.**
MBSR improves emotional regulation, reduces anxiety; increases cortical thickness.
PMC/DPI.
https://pmc.ncbi.nlm.nih.gov/articles/PMC11591838/

[13] **Harvard: Mindfulness Changes the Brain.**
8 weeks of mindfulness training reduces amygdala activation. *Harvard Gazette.*
https://news.harvard.edu/gazette/story/2018/04/harvard-researchers-study-how-mindfulness-may-change-the-brain-in-depressed-patients/

[14] **Brief Mindfulness Meditation Improves Attention.**
Even 10 minutes of meditation improves executive attention.
Frontiers in Human Neuroscience.
https://www.frontiersin.org/journals/human-neuroscience/articles/10.3389/fnhum.2018.00315/full

[15] **Benefits of Living Slowly**.
Slowness generates mindfulness; experiencing more through presence.
Psychology Today.
https://www.psychologytoday.com/us/blog/out-of-the-darkness/202407/living-slowly

[16] **Golden Ratio in Design.**
Mathematical proportion (1:1.618) found throughout nature and art.
Various (Mathematical principle).
https://www.britannica.com/science/golden-ratio

[17] **Individual Differences in Visual Product Aesthetics.**
Why well-proportioned pieces trigger positive emotions. *Bloch, Brunel & Arnold.*
www.jstor.org/stable/10.1086/374132

[18] **Amodal Completion (Visual Perception).**
How brains complete partial visual information; why certain forms feel 'right'.
NCBI Research.
https://www.ncbi.nlm.nih.gov/pmc/articles/PMC3188396/

[19] **Fibonacci Sequence in Nature.**
Natural number sequence appearing in spirals and growth patterns.
Various (Mathematical principle).
www.britannica.com/science/Fibonacci-number

[20] **The Psychology of Slow Living.**
Challenges speed culture; promotes mindful approaches.
Routledge / Elliot Cohen.

www.routledge.com/The-Psychology-of-Slow-Living-Rediscovering-a-Happier-Pace-of-Life/Cohen/p/book/9781032362236

21 **Wabi-Sabi Philosophy.**
Finding beauty in imperfection and impermanence.
Japanese aesthetic tradition.
https://en.wikipedia.org/wiki/Wabi-sabi

22 **Kintsugi: The Art of Golden Repair.**
Japanese art of repairing broken pottery with gold; celebrating flaws.
Japanese tradition (15th century+).
https://www.japan.travel/en/guide/kintsugi/

23 **Growth Mindset Research.**
Beliefs about ability affect learning; learning from mistakes.
Carol Dweck.
www.amazon.com/Mindset-Psychology-Carol-S-Dweck/dp/0345472322

24 **Acoustic Properties of Wood.**
Wood's sound properties; using sound as feedback.
Wood science research.
https://www.sciencedirect.com/topics/materials-science/acoustic-property

25 **Appearance Wood Products and Psychological Well-Being.**
Wood emotionally uplifting, associated with comfort.
Rice, Kozak, Meitner & Cohen.
www.researchgate.net/publication/279609818_Appearance_wood_products_and_psychological_well-being

26 **Creativity from Constraints.**
More creative outcomes under constrained conditions.
http://www.sciencedirect.com/science/article/abs/pii/S1871187122001870

27 **Rule of Thirds in Composition.**
Classical design principle for balanced composition
www.britannica.com/art/rule-of-thirds

28 **"Knitting and Well-being."** ***Textile: The Journal of Cloth and Culture***
Study of over 3,500 knitters found correlations between frequency and feeling calm, happy, and confident.
https://www.tandfonline.com/doi/abs/10.2752/175183514x13916051793433

29 **Evidence on the role of the arts in improving health and well-being.**
This comprehensive review found positive outcomes from craft.
Fancourt, D., & Finn, S. (2019).
www.ncbi.nlm.nih.gov/books/NBK553773/

30 **The Craftsman. Yale University Press**
Sennett argues that craftsmanship, the desire to do a job well for its own sake.
Sennett, R. (2008).
https://yalebooks.yale.edu/book/9780300151190/the-craftsman/

31 **Human Needs and the Self-Determination of Behavior.**
Self-determination theory demonstrates that intrinsic motivation
Deci, E.L., & Ryan, R.M. (2000).
https://www.tandfonline.com/doi/abs/10.1207/S15327965PLI1104_01

32 **Repetition & Variation in Motor Practice**

Practice schedules affect brain regions; deeper engagement.
https://www.sciencedirect.com/science/article/abs/pii/S0149763415002304

[33] **Flow: The Psychology of Optimal Experience.**
Optimal psychological states during creative absorption.
https://www.amazon.com/Flow-Psychology-Experience-Perennial-Classics/dp/0061339202

[34] **The Golden Ratio: Divine Beauty of Mathematics.**
Applying mathematical principles to design.
Gary B. Eisner.
https://www.amazon.com/Golden-Ratio-Divine-Beauty-Mathematics/dp/076036026X

[35] **Rule of Thirds in Composition.**
Where to place features on turned pieces.
Various (Design principle).
https://www.britannica.com/art/rule-of-thirds

[36] **Individual Differences in Visual Product Aesthetics.**
Why proportioned pieces trigger positive emotions.
Bloch, Brunel & Arnold.
http://www.jstor.org/stable/10.1086/374132

[37] **Entrainment and Motor Timing.**
How external rhythms influence motor behaviour and timing.
Psychology of Music / Repp & Si.
https://journals.sagepub.com/doi/10.1177/0305735612449507

[38] **Motor Synchronization Research.**
Links between auditory rhythm and motor coordination. *Frontiers in Psychology.*
https://www.frontiersin.org/articles/10.3389/fpsyg.2014.01185/full

[39] **Music Tempo and Work Performance.**
How musical tempo affects task performance speed.
Applied Ergonomics Journal.
https://www.sciencedirect.com/science/article/abs/pii/S0003687013000227

[40] **Stress and Decision-Making.**
How stress affects decision quality and pause strategies.
Psychological Science.
https://journals.sagepub.com/doi/10.1177/0963721411429458

[41] **Slow Craft Movement.**
Philosophy of working with natural rhythms vs industrial pace.
Journal of Design History.
https://academic.oup.com/jdh/article-abstract/28/2/173/345844

[42] **Pareto Principle in Craftsmanship.**
The 80/20 rule applied to finishing work.
Various / Quality Management.
https://en.wikipedia.org/wiki/Pareto_principle

[43] **Surface Science of Wood Finishing.**
Technical understanding of wood surface preparation.
Forest Products Journal
https://forestprodjournals.org/

44 **Natural vs Synthetic Finishes.**
Comparative properties of natural and synthetic wood finishes.
Wood Science Research.
https://www.woodmagazine.com/wood-finishing/finishes

45 **How design evolves through making rather than preceding it.**
Emergent Design in Craft.
Design Studies Journal.
https://www.sciencedirect.com/journal/design-studies

46 **Psychological research distinguishing perfectionism from healthy striving.**
Perfectionism vs Excellence
Journal of Personality.
https://onlinelibrary.wiley.com/journal/14676494

47 **Research on recognising cognitive fatigue indicators.** Fatigue and Performance Decline.
Applied Cognitive Psychology.
https://onlinelibrary.wiley.com/journal/10990720

48 **Neuroscience of skill stigmatisation.**
Procedural Memory Systems.
Neuropsychologia Journal.
https://www.sciencedirect.com/journal/neuropsychologia

49 **How experts make rapid intuitive decisions.**
Expert Intuition Research.
Sources of Power / Gary Klein.
https://mitpress.mit.edu/9780262611466/sources-of-power/

50 **Neural mechanisms underlying motor skill acquisition.**
Procedural Memory Systems
Neuropsychologia Journal
https://www.nature.com/nrn/

51 **Benefits of solitude for creative work.**
Solitude and Creativity.
Creativity Research Journal.
https://www.tandfonline.com/toc/hcrj20/current

52 **How learning happens through community participation.**
Communities of Practice.
Etienne Wenger.
www.cambridge.org/core/books/communities-of-practice/724C22A03B12D11DFC345EFC5DF9E0A7

53 **Studies on grip force and skilled performance.**
Optimal Grip Research.
Motor Control Journal.
https://journals.humankinetics.com/view/journals/mc/mc-overview.xml

54 **Relationship between respiration and motor control.**
Breathing and Motor Performance.
International Journal of Psychophysiology.
https://www.sciencedirect.com/journal/international-journal-of-psychophysiology

55 **Research on non-attachment and well being.**

Non-Attachment in Psychology.
Mindfulness Journal.
https://www.springer.com/journal/12671

[56] **Design philosophy of essential simplicity.**
Dieter Rams: Less but Better.
Phaidon Press.
https://www.phaidon.com/store/design/less-and-more-9780714849188/

[57] **How mastery leads to elegant simplicity.**
Expertise and Simplification.
Cambridge Handbook of Expertise.
www.cambridge.org/core/books/cambridge-handbook-of-expertise-and-expert-performance/

[58] **Comprehensive overview of Japanese aesthetic concepts.**
Japanese Aesthetics Overview.
Stanford Encyclopedia of Philosophy.
https://plato.stanford.edu/entries/japanese-aesthetics/

[59] **Cross-cultural evidence for simplicity in good design.**
Universal Design Principles.
Design of Everyday Things / Don Norman.
https://www.nngroup.com/books/design-everyday-things-revised/

[60] **Scientific explanation of wood colour changes over time.**
Wood Science and Technology.
https://link.springer.com/journal/226

[61] **The Japanese ethic of respecting objects and their lifestyles.**
Mottainai Philosophy
Japanese Environmental Philosophy
https://en.wikipedia.org/wiki/Mottainai

[62] **Protégé Effect. Research showing teaching improves the teacher's understanding.**
Applied Cognitive Psychology
https://onlinelibrary.wiley.com/doi/10.1002/acp.1556

[63] **Foundational work on knowledge we cannot articulate.**
Michael Polanyi (1966)
https://press.uchicago.edu/ucp/books/book/chicago/T/bo6035368.html

[64] **Research on knowledge transfer in apprenticeship.**
Apprenticeship and Tacit Knowledge.
Situated Learning / Lave & Wenger.
www.cambridge.org/core/books/situated-learning/6915ABD21C8E4619F750A4D4ACA616CD

[65] **Learning Styles Debunked. Research showing learning styles theory lacks evidence.**
Pashler et al. / Psychological Science
https://journals.sagepub.com/doi/10.1111/j.1539-6053.2009.01038.x

[66] **Multimedia Learning Principles. Evidence-based principles for effective instruction.**
Richard Mayer (2009)

https://www.cambridge.org/core/books/multimedia-learning/

67 **How reflection transforms experience into expertise.**

Reflective Practice.

Donald Schön

https://mitpress.mit.edu/9780465068784/the-reflective-practitioner/

68 **Research on metacognition and self-assessment**

Kruger & Dunning

https://psycnet.apa.org/record/1999-15054-002

69 **Csikszentmihalyi on natural rhythms in creative work.**

Creativity: Flow and Psychology of Discovery

https://www.harpercollins.com/products/creativity-mihaly-csikszentmihalyi

70 **Foundational definition of mindfulness practice.**

Jon Kabat-Zinn

https://jonkabat-zinn.com/about/

71 **Research linking craft activities to meditative states**

Frontiers in Psychology

http://www.frontiersin.org/articles/10.3389/fpsyg.2020.00266/full

72 **Psychological research on acceptance practices.**

Acceptance and Commitment Therapy.

https://contextualscience.org/act

73 **Teaching others enhances the teacher's own learning and retention.**

Memory & Cognition Journal

https://link.springer.com/article/10.3758/s13421-014-0416-z

74 **The culinary principle of preparation and its cognitive benefits.**

NPR / Dan Charnas

www.npr.org/sections/thesalt/2014/08/11/338850091/for-a-more-ordered-life-organize-like-a-chef

75 **Research on how experts must unlearn to continue developing.**

Adult Education Quarterly

https://journals.sagepub.com/home/aeq

76 **Research on specialists vs generalists and strategic depth.**

Range / David Epstein

https://davidepstein.com/range/

77 **How humility enables continued learning and growth.**

Journal of Positive Psychology

https://www.tandfonline.com/toc/rpos20/current

78 **Learning occurs in the space between current and potential ability.**

Vygotsky / Educational Psychology

https://www.simplypsychology.org/zone-of-proximal-development.html

79 **David Pye on craft traditions and continuity.**

The Nature and Art of Workmanship / Pye

www.cambridge.org/gb/universitypress/subjects/arts-theatre-culture/cultural-history/nature-and-art-workmanship

80 **How cultural knowledge transmits through practice.**

Outline of a Theory of Practice / Bourdieu

https://www.cambridge.org/core/books/abs/explaining-the-european-unions-foreign-policy/outline-of-a-practice-theory-of-translocal-eu-foreign-policy-action/9C4607E4ED97982829EB31440D214F4D

[81] Philosophical tradition on humans as makers
Richard Sennett / Hannah Arendt
https://yalebooks.yale.edu/book/9780300151190/the-craftsman/

www.ingramcontent.com/pod-product-compliance
Lightning Source LLC
La Vergne TN
LVHW010653110826
845149LV00014B/3075

* 9 7 8 1 0 6 8 3 5 8 1 2 8 *